THE
LITTLE
BOOK
OF
HORSE
RACING

ANNE HOLLAND

First published 2014

The History Press Ireland
50 City Quay
Dublin 2
Ireland
www.thehistorypress.ie

British Library Cataloguing in Publication Data.
A catalogue record for this book is available from the British Library.

ISBN 978 1 84588 819 0

Typesetting and origination by The History Press

CONTENTS

ACKNOWLEDGEMENTS

And my special thanks to: Jane Bakowski, *Kent and Sussex Courier*; Peter McNeile; Nigel Payne, Aintree Press Officer; Christopher Simpson; Jeremy James; Tom Walshe and John Warden.

www.aintree.co.uk
www.awchampionships.co.uk
www.bbc.co.uk/history
www.bettingbeauty.com/the-rise-and-rise-of-female-jockeys/
www.bettingsites.co.uk
www.bookiesindex.com
www.dailymail.co.uk
www.horseracinghistory.co.uk
www.independent.ie
www.jockey-club-estates.co.uk/newmarket-training-grounds/
    history
www.mirror.co.uk/news/uk-news/top-ten-betting-scandals-569158
www.newmarketracecourses.co.uk/
www.newzealand.govt.nz
http://paperspast.natlib.govt.nz
www.racerate.com/
http://theapprenticejockey.blogspot.ie/2011/12/druids-lodge.html
www.thefreelibrary.com/
www.telegraph.co.uk
http://en.wikipedia.org/
www.zani.co.uk/sport

1

HORSE RACING COMES TO BRITAIN

Netherby, Yorkshire *c.* AD 210 – the Romans have been in occupation in parts of Britain for nearly 170 years; they have redesigned a number of major towns along a street grid format with forums (market squares), basilicas (assembly rooms), temples, theatres, bathhouses, amphitheatres, shopping malls and hotels – and many of the former Celtic warriors and druids who now run these towns for the Romans have 'gentrified' themselves and live in the fine houses.

Now, in *c.* AD 210, horse racing is coming to a Yorkshire village called Netherby near Harrogate. Soon most of Yorkshire will reverberate to the poundings of racing hooves as the sport spreads. The new gentry are keen to make their mark, and before long they vie with each other to donate cash prizes, an early form of sponsorship, believing their social status will improve as a result.

Today Yorkshire remains one of the most popular racing locations with no less than nine racecourses, at Beverley, Catterick, Doncaster, Pontefract, Redcar, Ripon, Thirsk, Weatherby and York. There is also a prestigious training centre near Middleham.

FOUL RIDING

War was declared in the Arab world in the sixth century AD over an alleged incident of foul riding. The Prophet Mohammed intervened to end it a few decades later by drawing up race rules, regulating the ages of horses, the size of fields, and the distances.

It was to be a 1,000 or so years later, in 1619, that England introduced formal rules for horse racing covering, among other things, foul play and disqualifications. Other strictures were also brought in.

Matters became better regulated with the founding of the Jockey Club in 1750, and it remained the sole arbiter of the sport until 2006 when the regulatory side was taken over by the Horse Racing Authority (HRA). The HRA merged with the Horseracing Regulatory Authority to form the British Horseracing Authority (BHA) in 2007.

Today, worldwide racing authorities keep an eagle eye on foul riding and foul play of all descriptions, with rigid penalties right up to lifetime bans to deter would-be offenders.

THE SPORT OF KINGS

In the tenth century AD 'running horses' were sent by Hugh, founder of the Royal House of Capet, as a present to Alfred the Great's grandson King Athelstan (reigned AD 925–939, the first king of all England). Hugh wanted to marry the King's sister Ethelswitha. The King married off four of his half-sisters to various rulers of western Europe, so Hugh's attentions may not have gone amiss.

Henry II (1154–1189) described races at 'Smoothfield' (Smithfield, London) in which 'jockies inspired with thoughts of applause and in the hope of victory, clap spurs to the willing horses, brandish their whips and cheer them with their cries'.

Couplets penned during the reign of Richard I (1189–1199) refer to horse races taking place.

Edward III (1327–77) is said to have bought 'running horses' for £13 6s 8d each and was given two by the King of Navarre. Shortly before his death in 1377, his grandson, who was about to become Richard II (1377–99), raced against the Earl of Arundel.

By the time of Henry VII (1485–1509) a royal stud was well established.

Henry VIII (1509–47) kept a training establishment at Greenwich and a stud at Eltham.

James I (1603–25) discovered ground ideal for hawking and coursing by the New Market near Exning and this became

Newmarket racecourse. He built a grandstand and ran some of his own horses; he was followed by Charles I (1625–49) and Charles II (1660–85) who really established Newmarket as a racing venue in the seventeenth century.

Spring and autumn meetings were held at Newmarket around the start of Charles I's reign, and the first Gold Cup was competed for there in 1634.

The burgeoning sport was banned by Oliver Cromwell but Charles II not only restored it but was a keen participant. It was he who introduced the Newmarket Town Plate in 1664, and wrote the rules for it himself (see page 51).

DID YOU KNOW?

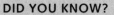

William Hill opened a book on a horse race in Ireland in 1690; at least one of the three contestants fought in the Battle of the Boyne a couple of months later.

The winner of the 1880 Derby, Bend Or, was really a horse called Tadcaster. The long-held rumour was proved to be correct in the 2010s by DNA testing.

In 1711 Queen Anne (1702–14) founded Ascot. One of George II's sons, the Duke of Cumberland, bred the two highly influential stallions, Herod and Eclipse, and the future George IV, as Prince of Wales, won the 1788 Derby with Sir Thomas.

The sport continued to flourish throughout the eighteenth and nineteenth centuries. It was recorded in James Rice's *History of the British Turf* in 1879 that 'for some two hundred years the pursuit of horse racing has been attractive to more of our countrymen than any other outdoor pastime'.

Queen Victoria maintained the Royal Stud at Hampton Court and her son, the future Edward VII, was a keen and very successful racing aficionado. He won eight Classics and a Grand National. He won the Derby three times, with Persimmon in 1896, Minoru in 1909, and Diamond Jubilee in 1900 in which year he also won the 2,000 Guineas and the St Leger, making him the only royal winner of the Triple Crown. It was some year for the prince because his Ambush II also won the Grand National. George V also won one Classic, the 1,000 Guineas with Scuttle in 1928; infamously his colt Amner was brought down in the 1913 Derby when suffragette Emily Davidson ran out in front of him; she died from her injuries. George V's son, George VI, won four Second World War substitute Classics with Big Game and Sun Chariot (see Sir Gordon Richards, page 80).

Queen Elizabeth II has been a lifelong racing supporter and knowledgeable breeder. Her first winner was in joint ownership with her mother, the Queen Mother, with Monaveen in the Chichester Chase at Fontwell Park, Sussex.

But flat racing became her greater interest and her first winner as sole owner was Choir Boy in a handicap at Newmarket in 1952. She has won more than 1,600 races and four of the five Classics, but the Derby has eluded her. Aureole was second in 1953 and Carlton House was third in 2011. Her Estimate won the 2013 Ascot Gold Cup, which resulted in her being voted Racehorse Owner of the Year by the Racehorse Owners Association.

Two of her children, heir to the throne Prince Charles, the Prince of Wales, and Princess Anne, the Princess Royal, have both not only owned but also ridden racehorses on the track. Prince Charles made his debut in the Madhatter's Charity flat race at Plumpton, Sussex, and finished second to TV racing commentator Derek 'Tommo' Thompson.

Princess Anne rode out for David 'the Duke' Nicholson in Gloucestershire. Her first win came on the flat at Redcar on 5 August 1986 and she also raced over fences with success.

It is no wonder, therefore, that, from the earliest times, horse racing became known as the Sport of Kings.

THE FIRST STEEPLECHASE

In 1752 two keen hunting Irishmen in County Cork each boasted that their horse was better than the other's. They decided to prove who was correct by racing from St John's church, Buttevant, to the distant steeple of St Mary's church, Doneraile, some 5 miles away. This would be no ordinary flat race, but they would negotiate whatever obstacles confronted them as they made their way from point to point. They wagered a cask of wine on the outcome.

Thus were born the joined-at-the-hip sports of steeplechasing and its amateur twin point-to-pointing.

On the appointed day many people congregated to witness the race between Cornelius O'Callaghan and Edmund Blake as they set off on what was to prove a momentous occasion. Starting with their backs to St John's church, they set off down the hill and over the River Awbeg, probably jumping fallen logs. They galloped up the hill on the far side where they reached a boreen, a sunken lane; they jumped off the bank into it, then immediately leapt up the bank on the far side to get out of it. Here the Cahrimee opened up into open farmland and more boreens, skirting boggy ground and on to a number of stone walls. They crossed another loop in the river, the church of St Mary's now plainly visible, ducked under willows, crashed through thick undergrowth and spurred their mounts on to the end.

Posterity does not record which of the two gentlemen won, yet somehow that is fitting, for they deserve to share equally the role they played in the birth of steeplechasing.

THE GRAND NATIONAL

Eighty-seven years after that first steeplechase the inaugural Grand National took place at Aintree, and in 2014 the most famous steeplechase in the world had a prize fund of £1 million – a far cry from the cask of wine that was competed for by Messrs Blake and O'Calleghan in 1752. Victory in 2014 went to Pineau De Re. The first winner, in 1839, was the appropriately named Lottery, for the race has always had an element of chance about it, although it only became a handicap in 1843.

It did not always have only large, fearsome fences. In the early years, most of the jumps were little 2ft banks topped with a bit of gorse and faced by a small ditch. The last two fences were ordinary sheep hurdles, but there were three – a 5ft stone wall in front of the stands, Brook Number One and Brook Number Two – that were huge. The first brook was dammed, making the water 8ft wide with a 3ft 6in timber paling in front of it, jumped out of deep plough.

It was into this that one Captain Martin Becher fell in the very first running of the race, immortalising the obstacle with his name. The second big brook, for the record, was the one known today as Valentine's.

For its first 100 years the Grand National was the pinnacle of the steeplechasing calendar and the one race all owners aspired to win. However, once the Cheltenham Gold Cup was introduced in 1924 that soon took over the mantle for top honours, because it is run on a level playing field, i.e. all horses carry the same weight, thereby giving them an equal chance of winning and decreasing the chance of luck, good or bad, playing a part in the result. The

Grand National, however, remains the world's most famous race, and more bets are probably wagered on it than any other.

Right from the start there were those that decried it, from the very first race when a horse called Dictator died.

Much has been done over the years to modify the fences, beginning in 1841, its third running, when the 5ft high stone wall in front of the stands was removed and replaced by the water jump 10ft wide and 3ft deep, with a thorn fence on the take off side.

The wall found its way back in 1843 but only for one year, after which it was gone for good, even though its height had been reduced to 4ft and was padded with turf on top. It is the water jump that remains today as the spectacle right in front of the stands. The water is 9ft 6in wide and 6in deep, faced by birch that stands 2ft 9in high. The shallow water is another safety feature, with a gentle slope to the far side turf instead of a lip; this prevents a horse tripping up if it lands just short of clearing the water.

Over the first 100 years the fences became uniformly big. The bases were made from upright stakes and growing thorn until 2013, and they are dressed with spruce, making them look different to the usual birch fences which are faced with gorse – or these days sometimes green plastic instead. From 2014 the inside of all the fences are now made from plastic and birch, making them more pliable and 'softer'.

The early National fences were very upright, making it difficult for a horse to judge its take off. A number of them have a drop on landing, notably Becher's Brook, the Canal Turn is set at a right-angle, probably unique in steeplechasing. The Chair is the biggest fence of all, standing at 5ft 3in high with a 6ft wide open ditch in front of it. The chair has seen just three equine fatalities since 1839, and the death of jockey Joseph Wynne is 1862. It is also the fence at which jockey Paddy Farrell broke his back and was paralysed in 1966 which, along with a similar injury to Tim Brookshaw soon afterwards, led to the founding of the Injured Jockeys Fund.

The most famous Aintree fence is Becher's Brook, not for its height, but for the big drop on landing (that is, the ground is considerably lower on the landing side than on take off.) Originally the drop was some 3ft on the inside, and a few inches less on the outside leading the inside to be called 'the brave man's route'. To have a horse soar over such a fence is truly like flying; but if it makes a mistake the drop will catch him out and he may well fall. Unfortunately, the landing sloped back towards the brook itself and this proved an added hazard for a fallen horse.

The first modification to Becher's Brook came in 1954, when the drop was reduced but major changes were made for the 1999 running after a particularly unfortunate mishap the previous year when a fallen horse slipped back into the brook and drowned; it had broken its shoulder so it would have been humanely put down anyway.

After this, the sharply sloped ground leading into the brook on the landing side was levelled off significantly. The brook itself was raised by 30in to include only an inch of water and the outside running rails were splayed out to allow more room for horses landing wide.

DID YOU KNOW?

The Derby could have been called the Bunbury – the name was decided on the toss of a coin. Lord (Charles) Bunbury lost, but got the last laugh because his horse Diomed won the 1780 inaugural running.

The skeleton of Eclipse is on permanent display in the National Horse Racing Museum (loaned from the Royal Veterinary College).

The skeleton of Arkle was dug up from its resting place to be displayed at the Horse Racing Museum at the Irish National Stud in County Kildare.

After a big pile-up at the fence in 2004, where some horses again slipped back into the by then almost dry brook, 2005 saw the brook completely re-modelled and covered in rubber matting. The first major change to the fences in general came in 1961 when 'skirts' were added on the take-off side; the size of the fences remained unchanged but the sloped skirt on the lower half of the fence gave horses a ground line.

In 2012, following increased pressure from various groups, the most substantial alterations to date were made. The drop at Becher's Brook was reduced by between 4 and 5in. This left the drop about 10in on the inside of the course and 6in on the outer – a far cry from the 3ft drop of a century before.

In addition the landing side of the first fence was levelled to remove minor contours, and the height of the fourth fence was reduced by 2in to 4ft 10in. All the take-off boards were increased in height to 14in.

In 2014 no horses were seriously injured for the second year in a row. Press Officer Nigel Payne said this was a great tribute to the sophisticated safety measures introduced.

2

INFLUENTIAL STALLIONS

Racing in Britain prior to the end of the seventeenth/early eighteenth century was between 'common' horses, bred to fight in war, to work on the soil or to pull carriages. It was the introduction of three particular Middle Eastern stallions, who were built more lightly and were faster, to breed with the English mares that began the foundation of the thoroughbred racehorse as we know it today. The three were the Byerley Turk, himself a warhorse, the Godolphin Arabian and the Darley Arabian.

Many Arabian horses, and Turkish horses, too, were imported to England between 1660 and 1750, but it is the direct descendants of the three foundation stallions that contributed the most to the breed through three of their descendants: Herod (The Byerley Turk), Eclipse (The Darley Arabian), and Matchem (The Godolphin Arabian, sometimes called Barb).

BYERLEY TURK

Standing at least 16 hands high, the Byerley Turk was not only bigger than the two Arabians that were to follow him into thoroughbred history a few years later, but he would also have been taller and finer than most English horses of the time. Unlike the Godolphin (14.1½ hands high), and Darley (15 hands high) Arabians he had a long back, plenty of bone and masses of heart room (as did both Eclipse and Arkle in later years). Above his elegant neck was a beautiful head with long ears, big eyes, and a commanding 'look at me' presence.

A deciding battle between the Protestant Williamites and the Catholic Jacobeans was to be fought on the banks of the Boyne at Oldbridge, near Drogheda, in July 1690.

Two years earlier, Byerley, aged 28, had risen to the rank of lieutenant-colonel and by that 1690 date of destiny he would have known how good the Turkish horse beneath him was. He may have spent most of 1689 in Ulster, and possibly took part in the siege of Carrickfergus Castle.

A year later, in March, he stopped off in Downpatrick, and while there he and two other officers decided to race their horses against each other. It could have been just another race between officers but for two things: one of the participants, the Byerley Turk, would be remembered for posterity; and King William was to lend his name – and money – to it.

The Byerley Turk was already well known in Hounslow Barracks and Whitehall Palace stables and was considered something of a mascot in England.

It is believed that Lt-Col Byerley and his opponents, possibly Col Heyford's Barb (Royal Dragoons) and Major Hamilton's borrowed cob (20th Lancashire Fusiliers), started their race from the crossroads outside the Flying Horse pub, Downpatrick. Soldiers from all three regiments, having heard of the event, went absent without leave to support and wager on their respective leaders; a man called William Hill, believed to be the forebear of he whose betting shops are a household name today – opened up a book.

The contestants were not allowed to whip or unhorse or use swords against each other. Spectators were not allowed to throw missiles at them, and the race was to be run on a clean circuit that the contestants had walked in advance; it was probably in the region of 3 miles. One source puts Col Heyford's Barb as the winner and while that may be more reliable there is another story of the race that has come down the centuries as told by the Governor of Hillsborough Castle to King William and unearthed by Jeremy James, author of *The Byerley Turk*. It was said that the Byerley Turk arrived at the start awash with sweat, reared high into the air when the starting pistol shot and promptly galloped off in the wrong direction, to the dismay of his 6th Dragoon supporters. By the time he got back on the right course, his rivals were half a league, about 1½ miles, ahead, as they set off in what appeared to be vain pursuit.

Yet as the race neared its end it was as if the Byerley Turk sprouted wings; suddenly he galloped past the cob and was closing in on Col Heyford's Barb, and according to some reports he got up to win in the last stride.

It was after hearing this story, and learning that the race was short of a sponsor, that King William endowed it with £100 in perpetuity, and declared that the King's Plate should be raced for annually. It still is, and is usually run over 1 mile 5 furlongs at Down Royal.

The magnificent Byerley Turk died in 1714, at the age of 25, and is buried at Goldsborough Hall, Yorkshire.

DID YOU KNOW?

The Oaks and then the Derby came about following the success of the St Leger on Town Moor, Doncaster, organised by Anthony St Leger and first run in 1776. It allowed three year olds to compete for the first time and, judging it to be a success, a group of friends dining at Lord Derby's Epsom home, The Oaks, decided to hold a similar race for fillies. The new race was named after Lord Derby's home and it was his filly, Bridget, who won the inaugural running of The Oaks in 1799. This was also deemed a success, and so the following year, 1780, Lord Derby and Lord Bunbury introduced a similar event for colts or fillies, and that was when they tossed a coin to decide on its name.

GODOLPHIN ARABIAN

The Godolphin Arabian (or Barb) was born in Yemen, exported to Tunis and from there was sent as a gift to King Louis XV of France. It seems, however, that he might have pulled a cart through the Paris streets before one Edward Coke bought him for £3 and brought him to England. Coke died aged 32, and the horse passed to Francis, second Earl of Godolphin.

To begin with, because he was considered too small, he was employed as a 'teaser' at stud – testing to see if a mare was ready, and if she was, she was immediately taken off to the intended stallion. But a mare called Roxanna rejected the main man, so the Godolphin Arabian was given his chance and, far from spurning him, Roxanna produced one of the era's great horses, Lath (nine wins from nine runs).

A second mating with this mare produced another good horse, Cade, and finally, best of all, Regulus. He was leading sire in Britain and Ireland in 1738, 1745 and 1747.

Today the majority of thoroughbred horses' sire lines trace to the Darley Arabian (and the Byerley Turk line is in some danger of dying out). Many famous past American horses trace their sire line back to the Godolphin Arabian, including Seabiscuit, Man o' War, War Admiral, and the dual Breeders' Cup Classic winner Tiznow.

The Godolphin Arabian died at Hog-Magog, Cambridgeshire, in 1753, aged around 29. The horse's grave in the stable block of Wadlebury House can be visited. When he was interred, the occasion was marked with ale and cake.

DARLEY ARABIAN

The Darley Arabian was secretly imported to England from Syria in 1704. He was reared in the desert outside Aleppo, among the herds and tents of the Fedan Bedouins, where he already had a name, either Manak or Manica, probably from the Muniqui line of Arabians renowned for their speed; one wonders why his name was not retained in England.

He was owned by Sheikh Mirza II, and the fine bay colt caught the attention of the British Consul, Thomas Darley, a merchant and member of a local hunting club. One story says that Darley arranged for the purchase of the yearling colt for 300 gold sovereigns for his brother Richard. Thomas Darley then learned that the Sheikh had reneged on the deal, claiming he couldn't bear to part with his finest colt. Doubtless, Thomas Darley felt that a deal was a deal. He arranged with some sailors to acquire the colt by their own means and smuggle him out via Smyrna (an ancient city located in Turkey), and that is apparently how the young stallion arrived in England, as a 4-year-old in 1704, to take up stud duties at the Darley family estate, Aldby Hall, near Leeds.

The colt, now known as the Darley Arabian, stood 15 hands high and was the lightest in colour of the three founders, with considerable white on him; portraits show him as extremely elegant with a long, fine head, white blaze and two white socks on his hind legs and a snip of white on a front one.

Once in Yorkshire, the colt embarked on stud duties mainly for his owner, but a local mare, Betty Leedes (by Old Careless), was allowed to visit him. She produced Flying Childers (six wins from six runs, three of them walk-overs) and the unraced Bartlet's Childers, champion sire in 1742. Old Careless was a chestnut with two white hind legs and a white blaze.

It is through this Childers line that the Darley Arabian became the great-great-grandsire of Eclipse, by Marske, born 1750. It might never have been, for Marske's sire, Squirt, suffered from the painful foot condition, laminitis, and the owner, John Hutton, instructed that he be put down but the groom intervened and saved the horse.

Marske was bred by Hutton at Marske Hall, Yorkshire (many of the early notable breeders were in the north of England) but he exchanged him as a foal for an Arabian of the Duke of Cumberland's. On the track Marske won the 1754 Jockey Club Plate in Newmarket and a 300 guineas match, but did not win again and was retired to stud two years later at a low fee. He stood at the Duke's stud until his owner died in 1765, and he was part of the dispersal sale.

BASTO

Basto, a colt born in 1702 and probably one of the Byerley Turk's last foals, was to prove one of his best. Like his father, Basto was nearly black, and not only was he a good racehorse, but also a good sire. However, probably the most influential son of the Byerley Turk was Jigg, who in turn sired Partner, and it was Partner's son, Tartar, who sired Herod.

HEROD

Foaled in 1758, Herod was owned and bred by Prince William Augustus, the Duke of Cumberland, third son of King George II. Herod, or King Herod as he was sometimes known, was reared at the Duke's Cranbourne Lodge, Windsor Great Park. The Duke, incredibly, also bred Eclipse, the pair being two of the best and most influential sires of the thoroughbred.

Herod won most of his races over the then normal 4 miles, at Newmarket and Ascot, beginning as a 5-year-old. At stud he established the importance of the Byerley line through many notable descendants, including the inaugural Epsom Derby winner, Diomed, who was by Florizel (sixteen wins from twenty-three races) in 1780. Herod also sired Highflyer, unbeaten in 14 races and whose sons were champion stallions twenty-three times in twenty-five years. Herod was himself the leading sire in Great Britain eight times, from 1777 to 1784, at which point his son Highflyer took over, and in time his, Sir Peter Teazle, also went on to lead the list a number of times, up to 1809.

ECLIPSE

Eclipse may have been foaled during the eclipse of 1 April 1764 (or in March, according to some accounts); he was certainly named because of it. He was a great-great-grandson of the Darley Arabian, born 1700, on the sire side, while his dam, Spiletta, was by Regulus, an unbeaten son of the third foundation sire, the Godolphin Arabian.

Eclipse was a bright chestnut with one long white stocking on a hind leg, and a white blaze down his head. It was this distinctive marking that led to the secret of his ability being let out by a woman walking on Epsom Downs; he had been worked so early that it was before any touts were watching, and his connections hoped he would make a winning debut at a long price, but when asked by the late-arriving touts, the woman told them she had seen, 'a horse with white legs, running away at a monstrous rate, and another horse a great way behind, trying to run after him; but she was sure he would never catch the white-legged horse, if they ran to the world's end' (*Eclipse*, Nicholas Clee, 2009).

Eclipse was unbeaten on the racecourse but was never champion sire, finishing second no less than 11 times, usually to his stable companion Herod. But his influence on thoroughbred breeding was equally great, if not more so – and his racing record was impeccable.

While a select few others in history have been able to match his race record, it is at stud that Eclipse became immortalised. He sired an astonishing 862 winners, and today some 90-plus per cent of thoroughbreds trace to him in their tail male line.

3

OWNING A RACEHORSE

While royalty and nobility and the wealthy still own many racehorses (and contribute a great deal to the sport) these days the man-in-the-street can be involved with ownership too, thanks to syndicates and clubs.

SYNDICATES

Today racehorse ownership involves a broad spectrum of people, with syndicates being popular. In this way, costs are spread around a number of joint owners; they will have 'a leg of a horse' – or even a tail-hair of one.

I remember the first ever syndicate horse because it ran under the name of my home town, Tunbridge Wells. However, his was such a success story that syndication became banned for a good many years after him, due, I believe, to 'security concerns'. Happily this is no longer the case.

I was still at school, but was later to work for the *Kent and Sussex Courier* whose sports editor Frank Rushford brokered the deal with local trainer Britt Gallup and his head girl Gill Porter (who married future top jockey Paul Kelleway).

In March 2013, his exploits were recalled by *Kent and Sussex Courier* reporter Jane Bakowski:

Once upon a time, Tunbridge Wells owned a racehorse.

Bought in January 1963 by 700 local subscribers who had each purchased shares of £5 or £10, the handsome chestnut gelding with its distinctive white flash raced in the town's colours of blue and gold at Kempton, Plumpton and many other famous tracks.

The notion of a town buying a horse was a novel idea – Tunbridge Wells was the first in the country – and brought the nation's press to the town in droves, keen to sniff out the story behind it.

It began, like many strange tales, in a bar. *Courier* sports editor Frank Rushford, a self-confessed 'racing nut', was chatting to Eridge trainer Britt Gallup when he began to wonder why towns did not buy their own racehorses and compete against each other.

When Gallup pointed out National Hunt rules decreed horses must not be owned by more than four people, the pair quickly came up with a plan to dodge the rules – they would set up a scheme allowing townspeople to buy shares under the stewardship of four 'official' owners.

It didn't take long for Rushford to persuade his editor, Frank Chapman, to leap into the saddle, and he was joined by racing fanatics Norman Pearson, landlord of the Rose and Crown in Grosvenor Road, company director Charles Judd and Stanley Hart, owner of Skinners decorating business in Camden Road.

The Tunbridge Wells Racehorse Fund was launched just before Christmas 1962 and brought an immediate response from punters, many registering using the *Courier*'s special coupons.

Within a month, Gallup was hot-footing it to the Ascot Bloodstock Sale with 525 guineas – £561 – in his pocket to cast a seasoned eye over the racehorses on offer. He returned home with Harwins First, and the *Courier* front page announced: Tunbridge Wells Gets Its Horse.

Standing tall at over 16 hands and boasting two recent wins, the five-year-old hurdler was rapidly re-christened Tunbridge Wells – alternatives like RTW or The Wells were rejected – and began to train at Gallup's Eridge stables.

A thrilled Norman Pearson told the *Courier*: 'He could be the town's lucky horse', while Rushford simply noted: 'Win or lose … the town is going to get a lot of fun out of this horse.'

Tunbridge Wells was ridden by the late Paul Kelleway, a National Hunt jockey who had worked for Gallup since marrying his head 'lad', Gillian Porter, a cup-winning horse-woman herself.

The first signs were not good – he began his new career with a fall, sending waves of despair through the town's unusually crowded betting shops – but by Easter the champagne was flowing at the Rose and Crown after he romped home to victory at Plumpton, cheered on by 500 local supporters.

Mrs Kelleway, who now lives in Spain, said this week: 'It's always a risk when you buy a horse – you can't look inside and see what the engine's like – but he was a reasonably good hurdler. He didn't compete at Cheltenham, but he won his races and everyone enjoyed it, which was the main point. I've no idea what became of him.'

In fact, the scheme had only ever been permitted as a trial run, and at the end of the year the National Hunt stewards decided it set a dangerous precedent; they ordered the horse's sale, and shareholders reimbursed.

However the impact had been felt way beyond the town. In a report thousands of miles away in the *San Francisco Chronicle*, writer Charles McCabe said: 'Newspapers picked up the tale, wire services sent it to the ends of the earth. The name of Tunbridge Wells and its healing waters got identified with an old human dream. Its magics were on lips in Hong Kong clubs, Miami bars and pool halls in Hamtramck.'

Perhaps it's time we bought another horse!

CLUBS

Clubs can now own racehorses along much the same lines as the original Tunbridge Wells. Probably the best known and most successful racing club is the Elite. Since their first winner in 1993 the club's horses have won more than 300 races, flat and jumping, including a number of group races.

When Soviet Song won the Group 1 Sussex Stakes at Goodwood it was the Club's 200th win. Dancing Bay won 11 races on the flat, over hurdles and in chases, including at Royal Ascot and the Cheltenham Festival. Early in the club's life, Mysilv won the Tote (formerly Schweppes) Gold Trophy, a valuable handicap hurdle at Newbury, and in 1994 Young Snugfit won a race at Aintree over the National fences.

Penzance won the 2005 Triumph hurdle at the Cheltenham Festival.

Remarkably, club horses have scored on every course in Great Britain. They have something like twenty horses in training for both flat and National Hunt at any one time. Members pay a weekly fee and apart from going racing they also go on a number of stable tours.

DID YOU KNOW?

When Dorothy Laird was appointed features editor for the newly formed Racing Information Bureau in 1964 she was compelled to use a male pseudonym, Charles Croft; at this time, women were still not allowed to hold training licences.

In 1966 72-year-old Florence Nagle, who trained with her head lad holding the licence, took the Jockey Club to court and won the right to train in her own name. She was soon joined by octogenarians Louie Dingwall and Norah Wilmot who likewise had trained for years in their head lads' names. When the Lady Jockeys Association was formed shortly after a series of ladies' Flat races was introduced in 1972, these three redoubtable ladies became honorary founder members.

OWNERS

I often feel owners are the most neglected people in racing; they pay the training fees and a percentage of winnings to their trainer, jockey, and stable staff; they pay towards a fund for injured jockeys (willingly) and they pay for various registrations, as an owner, and their colours (silks); they also pay vet's and farrier's fees and probably gallop fees as well. Yet invariably the recorded race results, with just a few exceptions, will give the name of the horse, trainer and jockey; and the commentator invariably names a trainer and refers to 'his' horse.

Some owners breed their own horses but the majority buy them at the auction sales, or more likely have an agent or trainer buy for them. The sales are a huge industry in themselves on both sides of the Irish Channel.

The vast majority of racehorses will not repay their owner's outlay either through breeding or purchase but, like fishing, hope springs eternal; owners will mostly be in racing for the love of it, for the atmosphere, meeting friends, and the joy of watching thoroughbreds performing on the track. Winning is a hugely pleasurable bonus.

4

RACECOURSES

What sets British and Irish racecourses apart from the rest of the world is their variety. Each one is unique; not for them the standard oval going one way round all on the level but they go left or right (or even both ways); some have sharp bends that suit handy little horses, others are wide open, suiting horses with a long stride. Some have steep gradients while others are almost flat. The vast majority are on turf, which means the going can also vary enormously; no wonder there is the expression 'horses for courses'.

There are fifty-nine licensed racecourses in Great Britain, and twenty-six in Ireland, including Down Royal and Downpatrick in Northern Ireland. Apart from Great Leighs, in Essex, (currently mothballed) and Ffos Las, in Wales, (which opened in 2009) all the courses date back to 1927 or earlier. The oldest is Chester Racecourse, which dates to the early sixteenth century.

ENGLAND

AINTREE

Home of the world's most famous horse race, the Grand National. Situated on the outskirts of Liverpool, forget about the vista and enjoy the spectacle. Today the Grand National is watched live by 600 million people worldwide. 'Ordinary' races are held on the Mildmay course. The Grand National meeting in April runs from Thursday to Saturday with one race each day over the Grand National fences. The Mildmay course hosts some top-class chases and hurdles and the meeting has become a festival in its own right, lit up by the scantily clad Liver birds, regardless of the weather. It is left-handed (L-H) with almost flat terrain.

ASCOT

Situated in Berkshire, slightly south and west of London. It is renowned for its Royal meeting each June, synonymous with fashion and the very best class of racing spread across five days. It has been a flat course since the early eighteenth century; National Hunt racing was introduced in the mid 1960s. Right-Handed (R-H).

BATH

Set on top of the steep hill above the beautiful Roman town. Flat racing only. L-H.

BEVERLEY

Just north of Hull, Yorkshire; an oval track, all flat. R-H.

BRIGHTON

Located on England's south coast in Sussex. Situated on the South Downs outside the Regency town, Brighton is flat racing only. L-H.

CARLISLE

Flat and National Hunt, on the north-west coast of England, just south of the border with Scotland. The Carlisle Bells, reputedly the oldest sporting trophies in the world, were first competed for in the sixteenth century, in a race that still bears their name. One of the bells is inscribed 'The sweftes horse thes bel tak' ('The swiftest horse takes this bell'). Races originally took place on Goteddsday (Shrove Tuesday) until 1609, and thereafter on St George's Day. Both were major festivals during the medieval period. Pear-shaped, R-H.

CARTMEL

Traditionally a summer holiday venue, close to the beautiful Lake District of north-west England. National Hunt. Sharp and undulating, L-H.

CATTERICK BRIDGE

Close to the army barracks, near Richmond, Yorkshire is flat and National Hunt, L-H.

CHELTENHAM

The headquarters of jump racing, set in a magnificent bowl beneath the Cotswolds and guarded over by Cleeve Hill. It has two separate racecourses, plus a now well-established cross-country course. It looks like a sweeping, galloping course from the stands, but actually parts of it are quite sharp. A downhill stretch three fences from home catches out a few horses, while the uphill finish thwarts even more when stamina is suspect. L-H.

CHESTER

Great Britain's oldest racecourse, it was founded in 1540. Set on the Roodee outside the city walls, by the River Dee, it is a tight circular track of slightly over one mile with a very short run in. One of its principal races, the Chester Vase, is a recognised Derby trial, run in May. Flat only, L-H.

DONCASTER

Yorkshire, sunny Donny, held on Town Moor, home of the St Leger, the oldest Classic race of all. Flat and National Hunt. Every year the winning jockey is presented with a hand-made embroidered Jockeys' Cap. For the last 20 years it has been made by 76-year-old June Robinson. 2-miles round, L-H.

EPSOM

Situated in Surrey, home of the Derby, and full of tradition with soothsayers and funfairs on the Downs (see page 112). A unique course with steep gradients and a sharp left turn, Tattenham Corner. The Derby is run on the first Saturday in June. L-H.

EXETER

Devon, a popular National Hunt course in the west country. R-H.

FAKENHAM

Norfolk, all National Hunt. Sharp, 1-mile round, L-H.

FONTWELL PARK

Situated in West Sussex, this is an attractive course whose steeplechase course is run over a figure of eight. The hurdles track is left-handed.

GOODWOOD

West Sussex, home to Glorious Goodwood each July, a stunning location on the South Downs. Flat only, R-H.

HAYDOCK PARK

On Merseyside, a little north of Aintree. It is a mostly flat oval of around 1 mile 5 furlongs with a slight rise on the 4½ furlong run-in; it also has a straight 6 furlongs. Flat and National Hunt, L-H.

HEREFORD

A flat track virtually within the city, National Hunt, R-H.

HEXHAM

Situated in Northumberland, close to the Scottish border. The Heart of All England hunter chase is run here (in spite of its name). National Hunt. Strong stamina text, L-H.

HUNTINGDON

Cambridgeshire, all jumping. Its Peterborough Chase in December has been won by top steeplechasers, including Best Mate. R-H galloping course.

KEMPTON PARK

Sunbury-on-Thames, Surrey, on the outskirts of Greater London. This course is home to the King George VI Steeplechase every Boxing Day. In March 2006 an all-weather course was introduced to replace its flat racing course. The National Hunt course is triangular and virtually flat with a run in of a furlong. R-H.

LEICESTER

A long oval with a climb to the finish, set in the city suburbs. Flat only, R-H.

LINGFIELD PARK

Situated in leafy Surrey. It still has National Hunt racing but introduced an all-weather course in October 1989, and hosts the winter Derby. It also stages Derby and Oaks trials. A triangular track, L-H.

LUDLOW

A rural National Hunt course near Shrewsbury, Shropshire. R-H.

MARKET RASEN

Lincolnshire, in East Anglia. National Hunt. R-H.

NEWBURY

One of the top tracks for both flat and National Hunt. It hosts the Hennessy Gold Cup in November, and the Tote Trophy (formerly the Schweppes) handicap hurdle. Among top races on the flat are the Lockinge Stakes and the Fred Darling Stakes. L-H.

DID YOU KNOW?

Racing took place on the frozen River Ouse between Micklegate Tower and Skeldergate Postern. This took place beside the frequently flooded Knavesmire racecourse, York, during the winter of 1607-8.

Epsom Downs, home of the Derby, is common land, open to all, but since 1936 the Walton Downs Regulation Act meant that the racecourse itself, the grandstands and the training gallops are barred from the general public.

NEWCASTLE

Located in Gosforth Park, Newcastle upon Tyne. This is England's most northerly track, on the north east coast. Flat and National Hunt. L-H.

NEWMARKET

In Suffolk (on the border with Cambridgeshire), it was founded by James I (see page 8) who built the first grandstand. It became hugely popular under the patronage of Charles II, who used to bring his court with him to conduct affairs of state while he enjoyed the racing – and the attentions of Nell Gwynne. There was a tunnel under the road from his palace to the Rutland Arms Hotel where she stayed.

Newmarket is in fact two separate courses, the Rowley Mile and the July course. Both have their own grandstands, paddocks, weighing rooms and other facilities.

Newmarket stages the first two Classics of the year, the 1,000 Guineas for fillies and the 2,000 Guineas. Flat only, R-H.

NEWTON ABBOT

Devon, a popular West Country National Hunt course. L-H.

NOTTINGHAM

In the Midlands, it is only 2 miles from Nottingham city centre, in Colwick Park. Flat only, L-H.

PLUMPTON

Nestled beneath a fold of the South Downs in Sussex, the track is a narrow oval, downhill on the far side and uphill to the finish. It was the scene of Tony McCoy's 3,000th winner. National Hunt, L-H.

PONTEFRACT

West Yorkshire, flat racing only, L-H. The last 3 furlongs are uphill. Racing was first staged in 1648. Originally horseshoe shaped, it was turned into a circuit of 2 miles 125 yards in the 1980s, making it the longest continuous flat racing track in Great Britain. It was the first course in England to have a dope testing facility.

REDCAR

Situated in North Yorkshire. Flat only from April to November. Racing began in the 1700s on Redcar beach. When a Mr Adamson charged for building a grandstand, he in return had to put up a bathing van as a judge's box, as well as the winning and starting posts free of charge. L-H.

RIPON

Situated in North Yorkshire. Known as the garden racecourse, it was founded in 1664. The course is a flat, right-handed oval of 1 mile, 5 furlongs. Sharp bends and undulations make it suitable for a handy horse. Racing in the town first gained national attention in 1723 when the city is believed to have hosted Britain's first horse race for female jockeys. R-H.

SALISBURY

Netherhampton, Wiltshire. Flat racing only, it is close to the beautiful city and cathedral which has the tallest spire in England at 404ft. Fifteen race meetings are held per year between May and October. There has been racing here since the mid-sixteenth century. Two historical racing greats won here, Gimcrack in 1768, and Eclipse the following year. In 1970 both Mill Reef and Brigadier Gerard won at Salisbury. R-H.

SANDOWN PARK

Esher, Surrey, it is one of Britain's top flat and National Hunt courses. It hosts the Betfred (formerly Whitbread) Gold Cup that brings down the curtain on the National Hunt season. Its major flat races include the historic Coral's Eclipse Stakes and the Imperial Cup. A right-handed galloping track, it has a line of fences, known as the railway fences, down the back straight that come in quick succession. R-H.

SEDGEFIELD

County Durham. This is an all-jumping course south of the city of Durham, L-H.

SOUTHWELL

Situated near Newark-on-Trent, Nottinghamshire. It was formerly an all National Hunt track but opened to all-weather racing nine days after Lingfield in November 1989. Frankie Dettori won the first race on the all-weather. On the same day Kim Tinkler became the first female jockey to ride a winner on an artificial surface in the UK, riding Tite Spot for her husband Nigel. National Hunt racing also takes place. L-H.

STRATFORD-ON-AVON

Set on the outskirts of William Shakespeare's home town in Warwickshire, this is a popular National Hunt track. It features

DID YOU KNOW?

Healing powers of the spring water at Epsom were discovered by a herdsman, Henry Wicker in 1618 (Epsom Salts are still known for their purgative qualities as well as for soothing sore muscles when sprinkled into a hot bath). Racing was taking place there at least by 1625 when a burial list referred to 'William Stanley who in running the race fell from his horse and brake his neck'.

Until 1950 there was still plough on the Grand National course at Aintree. In this year it consisted of a potato patch.

the UK's champion hunter chase at the end of the National Hunt season. 1 mile 2 furlongs, L-H.

TAUNTON

Somerset. This is another West Country course and like Newton Abbot and Exeter is all National Hunt. L-H.

THIRSK

North Yorkshire, this is one of the nine racecourses in Yorkshire. It hosts flat racing on its left-handed oval of about 1 mile 2 furlong with a 3-furlong finishing straight and a 6-furlong chute.

TOWCESTER

Northamptonshire. A stiff, undulating National Hunt track on a large, nearly square track with an uphill finish. One for stayers. Scene of Tony McCoy's 4,000th winner. R-H.

UTTOXETER

Staffordshire. All jumping, its principal race is the Midlands National, usually run on the Saturday after the end of the National Hunt Festival at Cheltenham. L-H.

WARWICK

Poses a fair test and is a useful pointer to big races to come. It stages both flat and National Hunt. L-H.

WETHERBY

West Yorkshire, 12 miles from Leeds. This is the only all National Hunt course in Yorkshire. L-H.

WINCANTON

In Somerset, it holds some prestigious trials National Hunt races. A galloping track, it attracts some top horses. R-H.

WINDSOR

Berkshire, just to the west of London and close to the castle. It has the River Thames flowing beside it. It used to have a National Hunt course until 1998 but is now flat only and is a figure of eight.

WOLVERHAMPTON

Situated in the Midlands. It used to be a turf National Hunt course but became all-weather in 1993; it was the first UK course to introduce floodlit racing. L-H.

WORCESTER

In the shadow of the city, by the River Teme. It is National Hunt. L-H.

YARMOUTH

Situated in Norfolk, it boasts a seaside resort and a holiday atmosphere. Flat only, L-H, and Britain's most easterly course.

YORK

Racing in York dates back to at least Roman times. The city corporation supported the sport from 1530. York is sometimes known as the Ascot of the North, and when Ascot was closed for redevelopment in 2005 it actually substituted for the Royal meeting. It also held a substitute St Leger in 2006. Its own principal meeting, the Ebor Festival, is in August and features the Ebor handicap and the International Stakes which attracts the very best horses.

In 1754, at the instigation of the Marquess of Rockingham, the first grandstand was built at a cost of £1,250 by the architect John Carr. New stands were erected in 1890, incorporating much of the

RaCING HUmOUr

Lester Piggott got off a horse at Brighton which had run badly and told the connections they should send him jumping. When asked why, he said because it had to be faster through the air than it was on the ground.

original building. A new five-tier grandstand was opened in 1965; the Melrose Stand was opened in 1989 and this was followed by the award-winning Knavesmire Stand, with additional conference facilities in 1996. In 2003 the Ebor Stand was opened.

For a while the racing museum was housed in York racecourse buildings, before it moved to Newmarket. An annual race for a golden bell was taking place in the nearby Forest of Galtres in 1590. L-H.

SCOTLAND

AYR

This is in the path of the Gulf Stream and as such is almost never cancelled for frost or snow in spite of its northerly latitude. It is home to the Scottish Grand National and Scottish Champion Hurdle, and on the flat to the Ayr Gold Cup.

Scotland's premier track, it is a left-handed oval of 12 furlongs including a half-mile run in. A 6-furlong chute joins the round track after just over a furlong. The course is generally flat, with gentle undulations, particularly in the straight.

HAMILTON PARK

Lanarkshire, 10 miles south of Glasgow. Racing began here in 1782 and is all flat, held from May to September. It became the first racecourse to hold an evening meeting on 18 July 1947. R-H.

KELSO

Roxburghshire, close to the Northumberland border. Meetings are held from October through to May. It is a sharp left-handed track, all National Hunt.

MUSSELBURGH

Situated on the A1 just to the east of Edinburgh, beside the River Esk. It was formerly flat only, Musselburgh took on National Hunt in 1987. R-H.

PERTH

Britain's most northerly course. National Hunt. R-H.

WALES

BANGOR-ON-DEE

Not to be confused with Bangor, a seaside resort on the north coast of Wales. A National Hunt course by the River Dee. There is a slope along the home straight that makes a natural grandstand for spectators. Triangular L-H.

CHEPSTOW

Home of the Welsh Grand National. This is a galloping, testing track with undulations along the back straight that make it a little like a switchback ride. Home to the Welsh Grand National just after Christmas. L-H.

FFOS LAS

Great Britain's newest racecourse, it is built on the site of a disused open-cast coal mine. It opened in 2009, and is in Carmarthenshire, west Wales. The track is a fairly flat oval of 12 furlongs, and is proving popular in spite of its remote location. L-H.

IRELAND

Most courses are dual purpose for jumping and flat and the two codes usually take place at the same meeting; there is a tradition for holding evening meetings. The Curragh is Ireland's only all flat course; Kilbeggan in the Irish Midlands is the only all National Hunt one, and since 2007 there has been the country's only all-weather track, at Dundalk, on the north-east coast. There is also, uniquely, the only official strand course in Britain, Ireland or Europe held on Laytown beach at low tide for one day each September.

BALLINROBE

An attractive summer-only course in County Mayo in the west of Ireland with a funfair atmosphere. Right-handed with some undulation.

BELLEWSTOWN

Another summer track, a left-handed oval.

CLONMEL

Right-handed set in attractive Powerstown Park with steep undulations; home to the Clonmel Oil Chase each November.

CORK

This course used to be called Mallow which is a town about a mile away; close to the birthplace of the first known steeplechase (see page 11). A flat track, it used to be prone to flooding from the adjacent River Blackwater but much drainage work has been carried out. The Cork National is held in November. R-H.

THE CURRAGH

Ireland's only all flat course and home to all five Irish Classics. The Curragh plains of Kildare cover nearly 5,000 acres of quick-drying, springy turf, making it 'the Newmarket of Ireland'. Its Derby day is organised with great panache and for many is a social must. R-H.

DOWN ROYAL

The bigger, more galloping track of the two courses in Northern Ireland; nearly square, its circuit is 1 mile 7 furlongs round. R-H.

DOWNPATRICK

Think funfair, think switchback; it has steep gradients and a short run-in, and a good atmosphere. R-H.

DUNDALK

This was a turf track until it was closed for re-development and re-opened in 2007 as Ireland's only all-weather track, flat racing only. It runs in conjunction with the greyhound stadium whose track is inside the horse track. Held under floodlights, it has become a popular venue for an evening out. L-H.

FAIRYHOUSE

Home of the Irish Grand National held every Easter Monday. Only a few miles north-west of Dublin, up to 25,000 people flock to it every year, many from Dublin and many for whom this is a once a year racecourse visit. The track is right-handed and 1 mile 6 furlongs in length.

GALWAY

Home to the Galway Plate, the biggest summer jumping prize in the Irish calendar, and highlight of the seven-day long Galway Festival. The last two fences come in a dip and are unusually close together, followed by an uphill climb to the finish. It is a tight right-handed almost triangular track.

GOWRAN PARK

In an attractive wooded setting, undulating and right-handed, it is home to the Thyestes Chase each January.

KILBEGGAN

Ireland's only all National Hunt track and a very popular summer venue. An undulating, nearly circular, right-handed track of 1 mile, 1 furlong with a short run-in.

KILLARNEY

This is possibly in Ireland's most attractive setting, with part of the Lakes of Killarney and the MacGillycuddy's Reeks in the background. Left-handed and almost flat. Attracts summer holiday visitors.

LAYTOWN

County Meath – although pony racing takes place on some beaches, Laytown races are unique in being the only strand racing sanctioned and run under the official rules of racing anywhere in Europe. Once a year, in September, crowds flock to the beach at Laytown, where six straight races of 6 furlongs and 7 furlongs are staged. The races are limited to ten runners, and there are no starting stalls.

LEOPARDSTOWN

Situated in County Dublin, this is probably the finest dual-purpose course in Ireland. The track is between a circle and an oval of 1 mile 6 furlongs. It is left-handed, with a slight uphill finish. It is home to the prestigious Champion Stakes on the flat in September, and holds telling Derby trials in the spring. It boasts a fantastic Christmas National Hunt festival as well as major National Hunt races in January and February. It races all year round.

LIMERICK

Situated at Greenmount Park, Patrickswell, 4 miles south of Limerick city. It was opened in 2001, and the galloping track is 1 mile 3 furlongs oval with considerable undulations. It holds a Christmas festival. R-H.

LISTOWEL

In County Kerry, this course lies within a loop of the River Feale and is accessed by a bridge. The track is flat, 1 mile round, and it stages a seven-day Harvest Festival each September of which the highlight is the Kerry National. L-H.

> ### DID YOU KNOW?
>
> Off-course betting was banned for the working classes in the mid-nineteenth century, sending the business underground. Credit remained available for the upper classes. Betting was either on course, via certain credit betting offices, or illegally conducted often in or around public houses, with 'bookies' runners' ferrying the bets from bookmaker to client.
>
> Betting had become a particular vice in public houses during Queen Victoria's reign. By 1938, it was estimated some £500 million was being gambled on horse racing in England according to the Christian Social Council Committee on Gambling.
>
> Betting shops became legal in 1961.

NAAS

County Kildare, an undulating mile and a half round circuit with a testing uphill finish. L-H.

NAVAN

County Meath, a galloping oval of 1 mile 2 furlongs with a testing 3½ furlong uphill finish; it attracts some very good horses and was the first course at which Arkle won; he also won his only flat race there. It is also where Dawn Run ran and won her first steeplechase. She is the only horse to win both the Cheltenham Gold Cup and the Champion Hurdle. L-H.

PUNCHESTOWN

Situated in County Kildare, this is home to Ireland's National Hunt festival that annually brings down the curtain on the season at the end of April/early May with championship races of the highest quality. A beautiful location and the chase track is 2 miles round, right-handed and undulating but not steep. The run-in is 3½ furlongs. The hurdles course is 1 mile 6 furlongs. It also features a cross-country course, and flat racing.

ROSCOMMON

Like other summer tracks, it is close to the town and well supported by local people. An oval of 1 mile 2 furlongs, it is right-handed with a slight uphill finish.

SLIGO

This is just 1 mile round, almost circular, right-handed, on the outskirts of the town. Summer racing.

THURLES

In County Tipperary, this is a stalwart of winter racing whatever the weather. The track is an undulating 1 mile 2 furlongs. R-H.

TIPPERARY

This is a flat track of 1 mile 2 furlongs, left-handed, and holds some top racing both on the flat and National Hunt, especially on its annual Super Sunday in early October.

TRAMORE

Correctly Waterford and Tramore, it is a seaside resort in County Waterford. It is only 1 mile round, with a steep hill up beyond the winning post and a sweeping downhill followed by a sharp right-handed turn into the 1 furlong uphill finishing straight. Races most of the year.

WEXFORD

In the sunny south-east of Ireland, there are races most of the year on its 1 mile 2 furlong track. A high draw is considered an advantage on the flat. R-H.

5

ONE-OFF HISTORICAL RACES AND LADY JOCKEYS

Once a year, on the third Thursday in March, the oldest continuously run horse race in Britain – and possibly the world – takes place near a Derbyshire village called Kiplingcotes, near Market Weighton.

It is not run under the Rules of Racing and it is unlikely to be contested by thoroughbreds because for one thing some of the ground to be crossed may be deeply rutted and therefore unsuitable to their fine legs.

It is believed to have been founded in 1519, when Henry VIII was on the throne. One of the rules is that it is to be run every year or it ceases. This has led to a couple of resourceful occasions, as in the dire winter of 1947 when thick snow meant there were no entries. So a local farmer, unwilling to see the race lost, led his horse the whole way through snow, ice and drifts.

There was another dilemma in 2001 when the country was in the grip of foot and mouth disease, and again just one horse and rider rode the course. A modern obstacle that, according to its two trustees, is putting the race in jeopardy is the cost of insurance due to health and safety concerns.

So here, then, are the basic rules:

- The course takes in 4 miles of arduous farm track and field.
- Riders must weigh in at 10 stone, excluding saddle, and horses of any age can be ridden.
- All those wishing to enter must gather by the starting post by 11 a.m. on the morning of the Derby.

- The winner receives the sum of £50. The second receives the sum of the entry fees.
- It must be run by 2 p.m.
- If the race is not run one year then it must never be run again.

Sometimes, if there have been sufficient entries, the rider who finishes second may receive more than the winner.

The race has become a local tourist attraction and a bus takes spectators to the course.

At about 12 noon riders canter from the finishing post to the start approximately 4 miles away. Spectators traditionally collect at the finishing post to see the weighing-in, the reading of the rules, and the riders leaving for the start. They then await the arrival of the runners, because the geography of the course and the lack of direct roads make it impossible to see the start of the race and then drive to the finishing post before the riders complete the race.

I am indebted to a friend of mine, John Warden, who watched the 2013 race and sent me this account:

Thursday 21 March 2013 saw the 495th consecutive running of Britain's, and possibly the world's, oldest horse race – the Kiplingcotes. Better known as the Kiplingcotes Derby, the race has been run every year since 1519 according to the present rules but is probably even older.

Run over a distance of four miles on public roads and tracks, the race is a test of stamina for both horse and rider.

The going this year ranged from good to soft, to bottomless mud and two feet of water, with stretches of tarmac thrown in for good measure. In near perfect weather conditions, 4°C, light breeze and bright sunshine, the thirteen riders assembled at the finishing post to enter and weigh out, before walking the course in reverse direction to the start.

Entries are only made on the day of the race, so there is no certainty as to how many runners there will be. Horses can be of any age and have in the past ranged from children's ponies to carthorses, hunters and point-to-pointers. Riders must weigh ten stone, without saddle.

For the second year running there was an accredited bookmaker present, which added to the excitement for the largest crowd of spectators yet seen at this event, forcing the local authority to introduce parking restrictions on nearby roads. Many of the estimated thousand spectators were able to take advantage of the free shuttle bus service from nearby Market Weighton, sponsored by the Town Council. Guy Stephenson, Secretary of the Trustees, said that he had never seen so many people at the race and that while he was delighted to see so many people the increasing numbers were causing problems with the local council. As this is a straight course it is impossible to witness both the start and finish – unless you are competing in the race – so the majority of spectators gathered along the finishing stretch to witness the climax of the event. However, the crowd was so thick that those at the finishing line were unaware of the approaching horses until the last second – indeed it was only after the winner went past that some realised what was happening.

The race this year went to Carolyn Bales from Malton on her seven-year-old, Woteva, who won by a comfortable distance. Second was Jeff Bridges, up from the Belvoir hunt, on Eeyore, with Jason Carver on Data a close third. For both the first and second it was their first experience of the race. An exultant but exhausted Carolyn described it as 'Mad, absolutely mad!' while Jeff admitted that it was much harder than he had expected, even after a full season hunting in the Shires. Speaking to me after the race, Carolyn said that she was left trailing by some 30 lengths at the start but was able to gradually make up ground over the first two miles, although she was still third going past Enthorpe and reaching the hardest part of the course. The track at this part consists of bottomless mud, deep ruts and pools of water up to two feet deep. By taking to the field alongside the track – perfectly legitimate under the rules – she was able to take the lead about a mile out and extended this to her fast-ridden finish. She said that she thought her horse was tiring after about two miles with the effort of making up lost ground on the leaders but seemed to get a second wind and pressed on when asked. Carolyn has been riding since she was a child of five but she admitted that this was her most exciting experience yet. Her horse, Woteva, a lightly built seven-year-old, had been given to her as a present a year previously.

After weighing in, Carolyn was presented with the winner's trophy, a silver horse statuette, by Lord Manton – newly appointed as Honorary Trustee of the race.

Official Result: 1, Woteva 6/4 JF; 2, Eeyore 5/1; 3, Data 6/4 JF. Distances: A distance, 2 lengths.

Eleven of the thirteen starters made it to the finish, two having come down in the mud and deep water, although both horses and riders came back unscathed.

The course: The course of the Kiplingcotes uses public roads and tracks to the East of the town of Market Weighton, on some of the highest parts of the Yorkshire Wolds. It is up and down-hill, mostly uphill and makes Cheltenham look as level as the outfield at Lords. The course starts on the Etton to Enthorpe road near the cross-roads leading to Kiplingcotes and is marked by the recently made starting post. The first two miles are all uphill, using the wide grass verges alongside

DID YOU KNOW?

France made bookmaking illegal in 1891; it runs the pari-mutuel, similar to the Totalisator (Tote).

Only a few countries worldwide allow bookmakers for horse racing. Besides Great Britain and Ireland, others include Australia, Belgium, Spain, India, Mauritius and South Africa; however, offshore online bookmaking has effectively opened up betting globally.

the road. After crossing the Goodmanham to Lund road the course takes to the tarmac, following the access road to Enthorpe Farm. After passing the farm there is a slight rise then the course descends again into the toughest stretch. The track here is bottomless mud with deep pools of standing water – impassable even to Land Rovers, the only vehicles capable of getting through are large tractors. Climbing up out of the dip the course eases off to just deep, rutted mud on the rise towards the finish. Half a mile from the finish horses and riders have to cross the main A614 road – this year temporary traffic lights were in place to stop the traffic – then a flat gallop along a narrow grass verge lined with spectators to the finishing post.

FEMALE JOCKEYS

When I was young it was my ambition to ride in the Newmarket Town Plate, not only because it was historic but because at that time it was the only race on the flat in which ladies could ride.

Eventually a series of flat races for lady amateur riders was introduced in 1972 and the first was won by Meriel Tufnell. Women had ridden in point-to-points in a limited fashion in Britain; they used to be allowed to ride in the adjacent hunts' ladies race which restricted them to approximately six race rides per year. Just before I started in 1966 the ladies' races became open to horses from any hunt, so it became possible to ride every week in the three-month season.

With the advent of the Sex Discrimination Act at the end of December 1975 women were, overnight, suddenly allowed to ride on equal terms with men in any race – including the Grand National. In January 1976 the first girls rode under Rules in both steeplechases and hurdle races (I had my first ride the following month, in a hunter chase at Lingfield), and by the close of that half season in May nine girls had ridden National Hunt winners.

In their first full season, 1976-77, thirty-four National Hunt races were won by women (mine was in a humble selling hurdle race at Stratford-on-Avon, but it could have been the Grand National itself to my excited family).

Since then, women have become established as a small but integral part of the sport, and there are some outstanding female riders on both sides of the water, among them Lucy Alexander in the UK who won the Conditional Jockeys title for 2012-13, the first woman to do so.

In Ireland Nina Carberry, Katie Walsh and Jane Mangan are household names; Nina has won the Irish Grand National (as did pioneer rider Ann Ferris), and in 2012 Katie Walsh memorably finished third in the Grand National at Aintree, the best placing – so far – of a woman in the great race ; she is sister of the masterly jockey Ruby.

Gay Kelleway was a pioneer on the flat in England, where Hayley Turner is a household name; she was the first woman to ride 100 winners in a season (a notable achievement for any jockey) in 2008, only three years after being Champion Apprentice. She has won two Group 1 races and has ridden in the Derby.

Amy Ryan won the 2012 Apprentice Jockeys Championship.

THE NEWMARKET TOWN PLATE

The Newmarket Town Plate was instituted in 1665 by King Charles II and first run in 1666 to be run 'forever'. Horses were to carry 12st and run over the Round Course of 3¾ miles.

> Articles ordered by His Majestie to be observed by all persons that put in horses to ride for the Plate, the new round heat at Newmarket set out on the first day of October, 1664, in the 16th year of our Sovereign Lord King Charles II, which Plate is to be rid for yearly, the second Thursday in October for ever.

The Plate was the first with a set of Rules, for example:

> Every rider that layeth hold on, or striketh any of the riders, shall win no Plate or prize ... Whosoever winneth the Plate or prize shall give to the Clerk of the Course twenty shillings, to be distributed to the poor both sides of Newmarket, and twenty shillings to the Clerk of the Race for which he is to keep the course plain and free from cart roots ... No man is admitted to ride for this prize that is either a serving man or groom.

It is run over 3 miles, 6 furlongs of the Newmarket Round Course, which runs 'on the outside of the Ditch from Newmarket … starting and ending at the weighing post, by Cambridge Gap, called Thomond's Post.' It is only used once a year for this race.

Competing in this race has never been about money – one of the prizes is a pound of Newmarket sausages and another is a voucher for Goldings, the tailor and outfitter in Newmarket High Street – but of women being allowed to race.

I did achieve my ambition to ride in it on our point-to-pointer/hurdler King's Rhapsody; I remember tracking the previous year's winner; trouble was, that horse only managed sixth on this occasion and by the time I realised it wasn't going to be concerned in the finish the leaders had gone; I think we finished sixth. If only …

6

BETTING

For as long as men have raced horses they have wagered on the outcome. As we have seen (page 11), steeple-chasing began as the result of a bet between two gentlemen out hunting. Flat racing, on the other hand, probably began through competitions designed to be part of battle training and evolved into races.

From the seventeenth to the early twentieth centuries betting gained a bad reputation because of doping and other disreputable practices. Racing authorities worldwide are vigilant in updating their efforts to keep the sport clean, but greed is ever present.

Until the beginning of the 1960s the ordinary man in the street had to go to the races in order to bet or use an illegal bookmaker whose runner would meet clients at an agreed spot. Only those with verifiable credit ratings could open an account and bet over the telephone. Other than that there was no legal off-course betting until 1 May 1961 when betting shops were finally permitted, and soon all the high streets of Great Britain had them; at first they could only operate behind darkened windows but this gradually changed, and in 1986 televised racing was allowed in betting shops.

Betting tax was soon introduced, in the 1960s, and racecourse attendances fell, so a change was made whereby people betting at the races paid less tax than those who bet off course to encourage people to go racing. About forty years later, when off shore online betting had taken a huge hold because they were outside the tax jurisdiction, land-based bookmakers' livelihoods were threatened and the Government's tax intake was drastically reduced.

A solution was found in the early 2000s with the introduction of the Levy Board in the UK, under which a fixed fee is paid by all bookmakers to the Government via the Board. This is reviewed annually, invariably upwards. It means punters no longer pay any betting tax on their winnings.

At present Ireland still officially has betting tax but in effect punters are hardly ever asked to pay it; instead, the bookmakers pay the tax for them out of their profits. A new Betting (Amendment) Bill is due in 2014. Once enacted, all online bookmakers and betting exchanges will be subject to a new licensing regime.

According to www.independent.ie, 'anybody taking a bet online from somebody resident in Ireland, no matter what exotic part of the world the company is operating in, will have to be licensed in Ireland.'

The UK and Ireland are two of very few countries worldwide which have on-course bookmakers, in addition to a totalisator. Other countries operate only a totalisator or pari-mutuel system run by racing for racing, whereas profits from bookmakers go to themselves; however, they benefit racing hugely by sponsoring numerous races, big and small.

The forerunner of the Tote was set up by Winston Churchill as a government-appointed board in 1928, with the intention of providing a safe, State-controlled alternative to illegal off-course bookmakers and ensuring that some gambling revenues were put back into horse racing. In 1961 this morphed into the Horserace Totalisator Board, and the responsibility for the redistribution of funds to racing transferred to the Horserace Betting Levy Board. In 1999, the Tote linked up with Channel 4 Racing to introduce the popular Scoop6 bet which involves bettors trying to select the winner of six televised races.

After about twenty years at attempted privatisation of the Tote by previous UK Governments, both Conservative and Labour, it was finally announced in June 2011 that Betfred had emerged as the successful bidder, for a reported figure of £265 million.

There are many different types of bets, from single bets to win placed on one horse, to a simple each-way bet (win and place on the same horse) and forecast (forecasting the first two home) to multiple bets in the form of accumulators (like the Scoop6), and a wide range of other permutations.

Traditionally, once a race had started no more bets could be staked, but with the advent of the internet and instant access to events there is now also 'in-running' or 'live' betting widely available in which the punter can place bets during the actual running of a race.

DID YOU KNOW?

In 1913 Britain introduced the Jersey Act, effectively reducing most American horses to half-bred status and thereby making them ineligible for British racing. It was not repealed until 1949.

The banning of gambling in many American states had led to a surplus of racehorses; many of them were exported to the UK and Europe. However, the papers for many of them, proving their pedigrees, had been lost in the American Civil War. England found a number of these winning their races, but feared they were not purebred. They were barred from the General Stud Book unless all their past parentage could be proved.

J.B. Haggin, an American breeder, had begun to ship large contingents of horses to England for sale, including the 1908 Grand National steeplechase winner Rubio, and the fear was that if other American breeders followed his lead, the English racing market would be overwhelmed. The American-bred Iroquois won the 1881 Epsom Derby in the hands of Fred Archer (see page 78).

The Act's effect was the opposite of that intended; for instance in the Second World War Britain and Ireland were unable to bring in French horses and it was feared this might lead to domestic in-breeding. The American thoroughbreds, meanwhile, were beginning to have worldwide success. The Act was rescinded in 1949, insisting only that for horses to be eligible for the General Stud Book they had to be able to trace back eight or nine crosses for at least a century, and to 'show such performances of its immediate family on the turf as to warrant the belief in the purity of its blood'.

This removed the stigma of American-bred horses not being considered purebred.

PROFESSIONAL PUNTER, ALEX BIRD

Alex Bird began life as a bookmaker; he became hooked on racing as a schoolboy in the 1920s. He discovered that his coal merchant father was secretly also a bookie, and in time young Alex became his runner. His mathematical brain led to him being offered a scholarship at the age of 14 but he elected to go full time into his father's business instead. He began studying the form and before long he crossed over from bookmaking to becoming a punter. He discovered that patience and planning were equally as important as form, jockey, going and distance.

He called himself an investor rather than a gambler. He observed, noted, and waited for the right moment; he did not bet on impulse. He learnt that where there was an odds-on winner he could nearly always make money by backing the second favourite each way. Soon bookies began to refuse to take his bets.

He devised a new method to beat them. He opened accounts with various bookmakers who advertised in the press. They would take up to four bets by telegram from any one post office. Alex Bird would write out the telegrams in readiness, all bar the name of the horse, wait for the first indication of prices to appear on his father's tapes, fill in his selection, then get on his bike and cycle hard to the post office to despatch them – all a world away from today's instant communications.

His system proved too good and once more the bookies closed in on him, either restricting his betting or barring him altogether. He was still a teenager, but he began employing commissioning agents to place bets for him.

One of his most infallible methods involved photo finishes. He discovered in 1948 that to the naked eye it nearly always looked as if the horse on the far side had won, but often it had not. So he stood by the finishing post, closed his left eye and kept his head still to see the actual winner; as a result he won 500 consecutive photo finish verdicts, making an average of £500 a time.

By the 1950s his betting had enabled him to buy a mansion, a plane and a string of racehorses; he also had a private dining room at Aintree and a box at Old Trafford where he supported his home football team of Manchester United.

By the 1960s Alex was regularly changing both betting systems and agents in a bid to outwit the bookmakers.

Betting shops became legal in 1961, and any wagers over £5 had to be referred to that shop's headquarters. Alex Bird would place bets of £4 15s each, using six cars and twelve men to place them in up to seventy shops, from 9 a.m. until the race start time.

He did not back on handicaps (the Grand National being his only exception) and he was making annual profits of 1.83 per cent on £2 million turnover. When a betting tax of 2.5 per cent was brought in during the 1960s clearly his sums did not add up. He scoured his betting records and discovered that he most often lost on 3-year-old maiden races, especially fillies-only ones, so he stopped betting on them and just about continued to pay his way.

THE BOOKMAKER

Betting on English racecourses may well have become a tote monopoly in the early 1960s, as it is in most other countries, had it not been for Old Etonian bookmaker Archie Scott. A retiring gentleman, he was forced into the public glare in his negotiations with the Home Office and the Jockey Club prior to the Betting and Gaming Act of 1960.

With his erudition and background he worked tirelessly to save the profession he had begun at perhaps the world's most famous school. He laid his first book at Eton and when Spion Kop won the 1920 Derby, the 16-year-old schoolboy only just managed to pay out his mates. When he went on to Cambridge, he found nearby Newmarket too tempting to ignore.

Born in Scotland in 1904, and standing 6ft, 6in as an adult, Archie Scott was a pillar of society – but when he swapped working in the City of London to take up bookmaking he also became persona non grata in upper echelons.

He recalled, 'My mother was a Victorian lady and it shook her to the roots. In certain houses, where I had been a guest, I was no longer welcome'.

Posh racecourses such as Ascot, Epsom and Goodwood would not allow him to become a member and they never relented.

He was passionate about horse racing and loved his chosen profession. He started off by working for Sidney Fry, then in 1933, the year Hyperion won the Derby, he branched out on his own. Six years later he teamed up with Dick Fry; the latter died in 1960 at the age of 96.

During the Second World War Archie Scott proved himself an unflappable leader of men; once it was over he set up A.C. Scott Ltd and, with his bookmaking partner Peter Shepherd-Cross, always lived up to the highest standards to become one of the most respected bookmaking firms on the English turf.

In 1960 his company was taken over by Alfred Cope which in turn was taken over by the William Hill Organisation eighteen months later.

Archie Scott turned his attentions to trying to save the profession. The Ante-post favourite for the 1962 Derby, Pinturischio, had been doped and the Jockey Club believed certain bookmakers were withholding information. A tote monopoly looked more and more like a racing certainty.

His relentless work was regarded as a milestone in the history of bookmaking. He worked through the era of Prime Minister Harold Macmillan as chairman of the National Bookmakers' and Associated Bodies' Joint Protection Association from 1957 to 1964. It was the negotiations of this body with the government that resulted in the Betting and Gaming Act of 1960. He also advised Home Secretary Rab Butler on the opening of betting shops throughout the preparation until betting shops became legal in 1961.

In addition, he was chairman of the National BPA (later the National Association of Bookmakers); he was a member of the Pitch Rules and Administrative Committee; a director of the Southern BPA; a member of the Tattersall's Committee; chairman of the Association of Rails' Bookmakers; chairman of the Bookmakers' Betting Levy Committee – and he was the first bookmakers' representative to sit on Field Marshal Lord Harding's Betting Levy Board when it was formed in 1962.

Archie Scott died from a heart attack in 1965 aged 62; his wife had been killed in a car crash three years earlier and a son on active service in Aden died shortly before his own death.

Tributes to Archie Scott were legion. The starting price reporter for the *Sporting Life*, Geoffrey Hamlyn, said:

If Archie had never lived there would probably now be no bookmakers at all, to the great detriment of the racing public ... but for his efforts there would almost certainly have been a Tote monopoly or worse ...

He will go down in history as the man who very nearly brought about unity in the bookmaking industry, a well nigh impossible task.

William Hill, who founded his eponymous betting chain in 1934 declared that bookmakers everywhere owed Scott a debt of gratitude and that the good things he did would live long after.

Archie Scott, he said, 'possessed scrupulous fairness and impartiality, he was the first gentleman of bookmaking; but for his selfless devotion and unswerving loyalty to their cause at a time when far-reaching political decisions were in the balance ... there might be no bookmakers today'.

7

CRIME

Where there is money there is crime, and horse racing has been no exception, especially in the mid-nineteenth century when doping was rife. Since then huge strides have been made in making horse racing one of the cleanest sports of all.

RINGERS

When you describe someone as being a 'dead ringer' for someone else it means they look completely alike. The term comes from the horse racing crime of switching one horse for another, usually a faster one, to win a race at long odds because the one it's posing as is inferior and unlikely to win itself. Sometimes paint or dye has been used to make the better horse look like the other.

I was preparing for a Kent point-to-point one day back in the 1970s when we received a phone call from head of Jockey Club security asking us to be ready to bring a horse away from the meeting at short notice. (He was a close relative, I should add, but I knew better than to ask questions.)

As the runners circled for a race for novices one of them, a strapping big chestnut called Red Keidi (according to the race programme) was beckoned out of the ring. An announcement told spectators that the horse had been withdrawn 'due to a passport irregularity'.

In truth, 'Red Keidi' was a winning steeplechaser called My Virginian. No doubt those involved with him had hoped he would win at a long price with their money on.

A better known 'ringer' in that decade was Gay Future in 1976; he actually ran as himself, but on the gallops he was substituted by a much inferior horse so that the watching touts would not think of tipping him.

> *Gay Future* was the racehorse at the centre of an attempted coup by an Irish betting syndicate in Great Britain in 1974. The plot involved a Scottish trainer named Antony Collins initially presenting a poorly performing horse at his stables as if it were the real Gay Future. This lowered the expectations of reviewers, and hence raised the betting odds on offer, when the real horse was entered in a race at Cartmel in Cumbria.
>
> On the same day, two additional horses trained by Collins were entered in earlier races at other courses, but these were withdrawn shortly before the races. Syndicate members had used bookmakers away from the courses to place a large number of double and triple wagers, which involved *Gay Future* in combination bets with these additional horses. The last-minute withdrawals now meant that a large number of bets would roll over onto *Gay Future*.
>
> As the race start time approached, syndicate accomplices at Cartmel ensured that the long odds (10 to 1) against *Gay Future* were not lowered by on-course punters. *Gay Future* won easily, but bookmakers became suspicious at the unusual betting patterns. A follow-up police investigation resulted in syndicate leaders being convicted of attempted fraud, although they received relatively small fines from a sympathetic judge.
>
> (Wikipedia)

In 1978 Cobbler's March won a selling handicap hurdle at Newton Abbot by 20 lengths; he was found to be In the Money, a horse which had won five times previously. This was part of a long, convoluted and in parts harrowing story that is fully told by racing journalist David Ashforth. The article can be found at www.thefreelibrary.com.

A horse supposedly called Flockton Grey won a race for 2-year-olds at Leicester by 20 lengths in 1982; in truth, he was an experienced 3-year-old called Good Hand.

DID YOU KNOW?

1896 saw the first, experimental use of tape starts at Newmarket. They were already in use in America.

After the First World War three sporting newspapers, the *Sporting Life*, *Bell's Life in London* and the *Sportsman* amalgamated to become the *Sporting Life*. The *Sporting Chronicle* was the new paper's only national rival. The *Sporting Life* folded in 1985 but in 1986 the *Racing Post* was launched by the Maktoum brothers. The *Sporting Chronicle* had folded in 1983.

The best-known ringing case was in the 1844 Derby, won by 'Running Rein' who in reality was the year-older Maccabeus. The Derby is open only to 3-year-olds, so the older horse was immediately at an advantage. Lord George Bentinck, however, suspected the winning horse had been dyed. He set off and visited every chemist and hairdresser himself between the home of the horse's trainer, a gambler called Abraham Levy Goodman, and his London club which he frequented daily.

His sleuthing paid off for he found a hairdresser who could remember selling a large bottle of dye to a man answering Goodman's description.

Horses are aged by their teeth, and Goodman had pulled out the horse's more mature teeth to make him look like a 3-year-old. He had spent two years meticulously planning his scheme. As a 2-year-old, Maccabeus had won a race easily but Lord Bentinck had caused an enquiry afterwards claiming it to be a three year old; the stewards found in favour of it being a 2-year-old.

The court case after the Derby was sensationally dropped when one of the men bringing it, Wood, found he had himself been duped. Mr Wood had been given the horse by Goodman in lieu of a debt, and believed its identity to be as given. The horse had been due to be brought to the trial but had 'disappeared', without Mr Wood's knowledge. Mr Wood was described by his counsel 'as high-minded and as honest a man as ever lived'.

The trial judge, Baron Alderson, asked:

> And why did they not apply to the police to have those guilty of taking him away, without such knowledge, apprehended for horse-stealing? If I were trying them for the offence, I should have no hesitation in transporting them for life. (Sensation.) If they had taken away the horse under those circumstances, it is no doubt a case of horse stealing. You cannot be expected to produce a horse stolen away from you.

At the end, the judge addressed the jury:

> Gentlemen of the jury. This is a case which I have listened to with a great degree of sorrow and disgust; for to my mind it is clear that a most atrocious fraud has been practised. I have seen, with great regret, that some gentlemen of high standing in society have gone and associated themselves with fellows infinitely below them in rank and character, and can any one wonder at the result. If gentlemen would race with gentlemen, then such practices as have been exposed would not exist; but if they will condescend to race with blackguards, they must expect to be cheated. You will find a verdict for the defendant.
>
> (Trove digitised newspapers, 1844)

The runner-up, Orlando, however, was awarded the race and stands in the record books as the winner of the 1844 Derby.

It turned out that there was another ringer in the race. Leander had the misfortune to fall and break his leg on Tattenham Corner.

He was put down and when a post mortem was carried out it was discovered that he, too, was an older horse.

Sadly the favourite for that Derby, Ratan, was doped, leaving him 'with his coat blue and shivery and standing in fright', according to an author called Sylvanus. The jockey Sam Rogers, who organised the crime, was warned off but the horse's owner, William Crockford, founder of the gaming club of that name, was said to have died of shock two days later.

CLEANING UP RACING

The trial gave the government the incentive to tighten gambling laws, enforce stronger administration and raid smaller gambling dens.

Huge improvements were made by Lord Bentinck, who was chief steward, assisted by Admiral Rous, who was to introduce the weight for age scale.

The new rules and practices devised by Lord Bentinck included the introduction of shorter race distances and larger fields; until this time many races were still matches (between two horses) over 3 or 4 miles. He introduced fines for the clerk of the course for every minute that a race started late; he began the practice of horses being saddled in a centrally located public place; and he introduced the number board displaying each horse's number, jockey and weight.

Significantly, he also began the red and white starting flags system, the white flag man to be placed down the track and to keep his flag raised in the event of a false start.

Gentleman riders (amateurs) were no longer to compete in 'important events', and professional riders' names were to be published in the Racing Calendar.

He also brought in a rule stating that 'the judge should be precluded from receiving any presents whatever from winners of races'.

All these new rules were published in 1850 in *The Laws and Practice of Horse Racing* by Admiral Rous.

DOPING

Although horse racing is one of the cleanest and best policed sports in the world, the lure of winning races and earning money means there will always be those who will try and cheat their way to success.

In 1812 one Daniel Dawson was publicly hanged at the Castle Gateway, Cambridge, for the doping of racehorses. He had an accomplice called Bishopp who used a syringe to administer arsenic into water troughs at a training yard near Royston in Hertfordshire. Dawson intended to back the horses to lose, but his plan came unstuck when the horses died before reaching the track.

During the first half of the twentieth century doping was usually bookmaker-inspired with doping gangs raiding trainers' yards to 'dope to stop' – usually the favourite. Even today a stable lad may literally sleep with his horse if it's hot favourite for an important race, added to which these days there are security cameras and instant communications.

Doping to win was also attempted by administering caffeine, giving the horse an extra 'kick'.

While doping to lose sent a notorious gang to prison in the 1960s, chronicled in Jamie Reid's 2013 award winning book

DID YOU KNOW?

Pony racing at Northolt before the Second World War boasted facilities ahead of its time, according to *Starting Price* reporter Geoffrey Hamlyn, including lifts and good class catering with reasonable prices.

Horse racing is the second largest spectator sport in Great Britain, after football.

Doped, it was a new form of doping to win that emerged in the 1970s through the use of anabolic steroids, the 'grow bigger and stronger' drugs.

At first they were not possible to detect in blood tests but that breakthrough came from the work of the RSS laboratory in Newmarket late in that decade. But such drugs reared their heads again in 2013 (see page 67).

In the 1980s there came 'doping' of an accidental nature when minute traces of a prohibited substance was found; this was caused by cross contamination of feed in big mills. It was possible for wind to have blown particles of prohibited substances, such as something as simple as cocoa husks, from one part of a mill to the part which produced racehorse feeds; or for an empty container to be re-used for racehorse feed, only for tiny traces to be detectable.

It was slightly different in 1979 when a horse called No Bombs won a hurdle race at Worcester. Theobromine was found in a routine dope test afterwards. The cause was a mystery, until it was discovered that the horse's lad had fed it a Mars Bar en route to the races.

SELF-MANUFACTURED 'DOPE'

In 1967 Hill House, who famously twice won the Schweppes (now Betfair) Gold Trophy, a handicap hurdle at Newbury, was found to have cortisol in his system. The trainer Ryan Price was interviewed by the stewards who accused him of having not run the horse on its true merits in its previous race and of being the trainer of a horse to which a non-normal nutrient had been administered.

Ryan Price, a former Second World War commando, faced being warned off for life. Luckily for him, and for justice, one of his owners, Lady Weir (who was to win the 1969 Cheltenham Gold Cup with What A Myth) contacted a cancer research scientist who specialised in the field of cortisol. Tests were also run on Hill House for nearly six months and it was proved that even the stress and excitement of travelling to the Horseracing Forensic Laboratory at Newmarket was enough for him to produce so much adrenalin that cortisol was found in his blood.

In later years Hill House was tried at point-to-pointing but he planted himself at the start and refused to race. (I once rode him in a canter at his west Wales yard, and I remember what a fine 'front' he had.)

Two important things resulted from the Hill House case, the first being that in the future the accused person could be legally represented, and the second that a threshold limit was introduced for certain substances that can be found or manufactured naturally in a horse.

STEROIDS

Doping reared its head again in 2013 when a scandal broke out in Newmarket. It involved the use of anabolic steroids with two trainers.

Mahmood Al Zarooni, a trainer for Sheikh Mohammed, ruler of Dubai, was banned for eight years after being found guilty of administering anabolic steroids, and in December Gerard Butler was banned for five years.

Al Zarooni, who won the Dubai World Cup – the world's richest horse race – for Godolphin in 2012 with Monterosso, as well as the St Leger and 1,000 Guineas, admitted administering prohibited substances to horses at the Moulton Paddocks stable.

Sheikh Mohammed's wife, Princess Haya, President of the International Equestrian Federation, ordered an independent inquiry, appointing former London police chief Lord Stevens to undertake it, after the British Horseracing Authority (BHA) inquiry.

Mr Stevens concluded that:

> Throughout our investigation of the three entirely separate incidents, we have established that no evidence whatsoever exists to suggest that HH Sheikh Mohammed had any knowledge of the purchase, transportation or use of any

unregulated medicines. Equally neither did he have any knowledge of the illegal activities of Mahmood Al Zarooni.

The Sheikh, whose racing operation is huge globally, said that while Al Zarooni had been banned from racing for eight years, he was banning him for life and the trainer would never work for him again. He added that the trainer had not doped them for racing but for long-term treatment.

He said that the import, sale and purchase of anabolic steroids and giving them to horses would become criminal offences in the UAE.

The BHA said the scandal, which caused serious embarrassment to Sheikh Mohammed, was a result of Al-Zarooni acting alone without the knowledge of his senior staff.

Gerard Butler had also worked on his own, without either his senior staff or vets knowing that he was injecting nine horses with a steroid that was intended for humans.

At a BHA enquiry he admitted to seven charges relating to injecting horses. The BHA called what he did an appalling breach of his duty to look after the interests of the horses in his care. He was given less than a week in which to disperse his string of horses. He had bought the drugs on the internet. They were ten times more concentrated than one intended for use on horses.

Butler told the enquiry that he did not think his owners would pay for the treatment.

In its ruling, the BHA panel said his behaviour in administering the injections was consistent with the 'underhand and covert manner in which he purchased the drug'.

KIDNAP AND DEATH OF A HORSE

Shergar remains one of the most impressive Derby winners of all time. He scorched away from his talented rivals to a record 10-length win in 1981, the 201st running of the number one Classic.

Not impressively eye-catching as a 2-year-old, at 3 he won two Derby preps by wide margins, leaving him to be installed one of the shortest-priced favourites in the Derby.

Far from letting down his supporters, he won, easing down, by a record 10 lengths, ridden by 19-year-old Walter Swinburn. Shergar followed this with victory in the Irish Derby. His first contest against older horses came in the King George VI Stakes at Royal Ascot, a race he yet again won easily. When he failed in the St Leger he was immediately retired to stud, bypassing the Prix de l'Arc de Triomphe.

He had one foal on the ground and another thirty-nine imminent when, at approximately 8.30 p.m. on Tuesday 8 February 1983, kidnappers came, so to speak, knocking on his stable door. Security was minimal and not only was it all too easy to take him, but it was eight hours before the police were informed; it seemed that everyone else with any sort of connection with the horse were told before someone thought of calling the police.

The saga is written up comprehensively in *Hostage, Notorious Irish Kidnappings* by Paul Howard (The O'Brien Press). It is widely understood that Shergar was kidnapped by the IRA and shot within days. It is believed that the gang members did not know how to handle a thoroughbred stallion. They had also failed to realise, when demanding a ransom, that Shergar's breeder, the Aga Khan, was no longer the outright (wealthy) owner of the horse, but that he had sold thirty-three of the forty shares, meaning that negotiations would have to be taken with an unwieldly number.

It remains one of the most talked about and saddest crimes in horse racing.

'STOPPING' HORSES

'Stopping' horses, or 'not trying' can be difficult to detect. The reason jockeys were banned from owning or otherwise having an interest in racehorses in 1887 was because a top jockey, Charles Wood, was accused of stopping horses and running a jockeys' ring to deceive owners and trainers and of cohorting with the bookmakers for his own profit. Second only to Fred Archer in his heyday, Wood owned several horses. In 1888, a year after the new rule came in, his licence was withdrawn.

In the early races at Chester the victors were awarded the 'Chester Bells', a set of decorative bells for decorating the horse's bridle, and from 1744 the 'Grosvenor Gold Cup' was a small tumbler made from solid gold (later silver). In 1745, the meeting became a four-day one, with one race on each day. In 1766 a May Festival was introduced, and in 1824 the Tradesmen's Cup Race (the predecessor to the Chester Cup) was also introduced. The racecourse was at that point still just an open field, with the first grandstand finished in 1817.

Races were also run for silver bells at Gatherley, Yorkshire, Croydon and Theobalds on Enfield Chase.

BEATING THE BOOKIES – LEGALLY: DRUID'S LODGE CONFEDERACY

For horse racing connections, Salisbury Plain in Wiltshire is best known today for the impeccable stables of Richard Hannon at Everleigh and Herridge. Richard Senior retired at the end of 2013 as champion trainer, handing over the reins to Richard Junior; Queen Elizabeth II is among their patrons.

Back in the early 1900s on another part of Salisbury Plain there was a secretive set up. It was the custom for touts to watch horses at exercise in Newmarket, to spot the most promising and to thwart them winning at big prices. A group of five gamblers set up training at Druid's Lodge (now a polo centre) out of sight of prying eyes a few miles from Stonehenge.

They masterminded a number of lucrative coups. Visitors were not allowed and stable lads were not allowed to mention horses' names in their letters home.

The confederates – gang would be too strong a word for they did nothing illegal – would buy horses mostly in Ireland with poor form, build them up and train them on the wonderful turf of Salisbury Plain and when they were ready enter them for handicaps in which, because of their poor previous form, they would have low weights.

The main reason they could win at long prices was because there were no touts to watch them on the gallops, so the word about their improvement would not get out.

In a book called *The Druid's Lodge Confederacy – The Gamblers Who Made Racing Pay*, author Paul Mathieu described the confederacy as 'an eclectic bunch'.

He wrote that it was headed by Percy Cunliffe, an Old Etonian gold speculator who weighted in at more than 20st and 'was not a man much given to smiling'.

The man responsible for 'planking' the money down was Wilfred Bagwell Purefoy. Called 'Pure' by his friends, he collected rare orchids, invested heavily in music hall, bred racehorses, and was a director of the Autostrop Safety Razor Company, a competitor of Gillette.

The funds were fronted by Captain Frank Forester, a dedicated huntsman who was 'a rather terrifying man in the early stages of a run'.

Another member was Edward Wigan, a small, extremely uncommunicative man, with a fondness for milk puddings who pronounced the word coup as 'cowp'. Another Old Etonian, he was criticised by one of his masters for 'only paying enough attention to turn what I've said into a Spoonerism'.

The quintet was made up by an Irish vet Holmer Peard, who oversaw the trials that the confederacy ran at their stables at Salisbury Plain. Peard had bought Sceptre and the unusually spotted and exceptionally speedy grey The Tetrarch. Sceptre is one of my favourite horses in racing history; a filly, she won four of the five Classics in 1902 and was unlucky not to win the

Derby. (Colts are only eligible for the 2,000 Guineas, Derby and St Leger but a filly is allowed to run in all of them; however, that is rare in the extreme.)

The trainer that these men installed at Druid's Lodge was Irishman Jack Fallon, and the jockey usually used was another Irishman, Bernard Dillon; between them they pulled off some outstanding gambles including in races like the Cambridgeshire.

Shrewd judgement, good training and lack of today's modern communication systems helped towards a decade of success, which only came to an end because of the outbreak of the First World War.

BARNEY CURLEY

The name Barney Curley is synonymous with clever betting coups. Bellewstown, an Irish track in County Meath that races a couple of times a year in the summer, was the scene of the Yellow Sam coup in 1975 for which Barney Curley will forever be remembered in racing circles.

Bellewstown had just one telephone. This was long before mobile phones or internet access. The plan was simple enough. Barney Curley saw to it that the only phone was permanently engaged; he had an accomplice in it talking to a fictional dying aunt. Off-course bookmakers tried desperately to get through as more and more money was piled on to Yellow Sam in their offices. They knew his price had to come down, but if they couldn't get through to their fellows on the track (where no such money was being put on the horse) the starting price would be way too long.

Yellow Sam duly won, and Barney Curley is said to have scooped a small fortune through his many off-course bets.

By the 2000s, with sophisticated communication systems preventing a repetition of the Bellewstown style, but doubtless allowing for improved contact with his associates, he brought off two known four-horse accumulators.

In 2010 he is said to have won more than £1 million in a coup involving four horses, three of which he trained himself, and he had previously owned the fourth.

Then in January 2014 he did it again, with four horses on three British tracks, in a four-horse accumulator. He had links with the four horses, all of whom had been off the track for between 225 and 700 days, an incredible training feat in itself.

'It's not for the money,' Curley said in a rare interview with the *Irish Independent* in 2010. 'It's for the buzz. Beat the system, you know, beat those bookmakers, those smart-arses. You go into a betting shop and see them robbing these poor fellows, with these gaming machines' (Declan Whooley, January 2014).

But there is more to Barney Curley, originally from County Fermanagh, than beating the bookies, much as that doubtless gives him huge satisfaction.

In 1995 he lost a teenage son in a car accident and he has devoted much of his time since then to a charity he set up in Zambia.

He is also remembered for disposing of his house, Middleton Park, by raffle. The fine house in the Westmeath village of Castletown Geoghegan is currently a hotel and popular wedding venue. The stables are used by trainer Martin Lynch who sent out Oscar Time to finish second in the 2011 Grand National for amateur Sam Waley-Cohen.

8

JOCKEYS DOWN THE CENTURIES

In the early days of British horse racing, owners tended to ride their own horses in races. This practice died out as racing became more organised and the owners, most of them aristocrats, had grooms ride the horses instead i.e. first professional riders. Jockeys at this time were often scruffy and unkempt and not well-regarded.

These days there are approximately 430 professional jockeys based in the United Kingdom.

The nineteenth century was dominated by three jockeys – Nat Flatman, George Fordham and Fred Archer – who between them won forty flat jockeys' championships. With the expansion of newspapers and the growth of interest in horse racing among ordinary people, these jockeys became nationally recognised figures, with the sort of profile that is given to footballers and TV celebrities today.

TOD SLOAN

Tod Sloan revolutionised race riding yet ended his days in ignominy. The end of the nineteenth century and the early twentieth could so easily have belonged to Sloan. Although he did not himself invent the shorter stirrups and low forward-crouch style for jockeys – that accolade goes to fellow American Harry Griffin – it was nevertheless Tod who brought it to England, only to be laughed at, and caricatured as 'a monkey on a stick'.

Not until he began winning – and winning and winning – did the racing fraternity begin to sit up(!) and take notice. He was well balanced on his mounts, and his low body position with his seat out of the saddle offered less wind resistance, making it possible to go faster than his upright opponents sitting down in their saddles.

Born in 1874 into a humble and non-horsey background in Indiana, Tod Sloan's childhood acquaintances were Buffalo Bill and Frank James who, like his brother Jesse, was a bandit.

Tod's first efforts at becoming a jockey were fruitless and he thought about quitting. However, he watched Harry Griffin's low style, one of the best and most underrated of jockeys. Tod thought about it and put two and two together. One day he was being run away with a horse on the way to the start of a race. He got up out of the saddle and lent over the horse's neck with remarkable results; he practised his new style at home and at last produced it in a race. Spectators thought he had turned into a comedian but he began winning races.

He also found that horses ran best when covered up (by other horses), so again there was less wind resistance; and also that they fared better when they had a running rail or a horse on both sides of it to guide it. He also gained a reputation for cajoling recalcitrant horses.

In 1896 Tom Loates, who was English Champion three times in 1896, '90 and '93, visited America and took Tod under his wing, tipping him winners that he was riding. The next year Tod arrived in Newmarket, homesick, with few friends and almost no rides. His 'monkey' style was ridiculed. It was the year tape starts were introduced, but Tod was already used to them in America and so was at an advantage. He wrote, 'When the barrier flew up and the others were getting ready, I was nearly a quarter finished!'

Tod was also surprised at how hard-trained the horses were in England compared with America. He considered a 'warm-up canter' that he had to do was more like a 4-mile gallop and was then flabbergasted to discover he was then meant to gallop the horse as well. But he was impressed with the way jockeys were treated, for instance being given luncheon vouchers.

At one time it was suggested he should carry a penalty because his style was 'unfair'. It was not so much his shortness of stirrup that gave him the advantage, he said, as the crouching forward, altering the whole balance and enabling the horse to use its speed and action to better effect.

Soon, his success brought not only recognition but also imitation, and before long all the jockeys were riding in the new style. He began to meet the good and the great, including the Prince of Wales, the future King Edward VII.

He never used spurs and seldom a whip, pointing out that 'hands and brain have more to do with successful race riding than anything else'.

One day he rode four winners in Manchester and he was nearly mobbed by his fans wanting to pat his back or shake his hand; it took twelve policemen to escort him to his waiting cab. He had ridden twenty-eight winners from his last forty-eight rides.

But dark clouds were on the horizon. Other American owners were bringing horses over and winning; there was unease and disquiet and fear of foul play among the English authorities.

Tod was brought before the stewards in 1900 and readily admitted when asked that he would back horses he was riding himself believing that, as in America, this was allowed. It was

DID YOU KNOW?

In 1740, the British Parliament introduced an act 'to restrain and to prevent the excessive increase in horse racing'; this was largely ignored and in the 1750 the Jockey Club was formed to create and apply the Rules of Racing.

The term gee-gee for a horse comes from one Henry Gee, Mayor of Chester, who after a particularly violent football match in 1533, banned the playing of the game and instituted horse racing instead, founded in 1539.

well known, he said, that many British jockeys bet 'and not all in half sovereigns'. He was reprimanded and returned home to America for the winter.

When he applied for his licence for 1901 it was refused.

He tried again for the next fifteen consecutive years until, in 1915, he worked with ambulances in the First World War.

Between 1900 and that time, he began a business with the newfangled automobiles but it failed; he won an action against the French Jockey Club but it cost him both financially and in his bid to regain his British licence.

In 1913 Britain introduced the Jersey Act, banning American horses that could not prove a pure thoroughbred pedigree; as the majority of records had been destroyed in the American Civil War, 1861–65, this de-barred most of them.

Tod rode in England for just four years and was cast aside for fifteen. He died in 1933 in obscurity – but his style remains the basis for jockeys the world over today.

STEVE DONOGHUE

The turn of the century heralded Steve Donoghue, forever remembered for his partnership with Brown Jack, winner of the Queen Alexandra Stakes an astonishing six times. Brown Jack became the most famous 'cup' horse of his day – or any other day, for that matter. He became a Royal Ascot specialist, yet remarkably he won the second ever Champion Hurdle, in 1928, before going on to make long-distance flat history.

Steve Donoghue and Brown Jack were genuinely fond of each other; it is said that the horse licked the jockey's face affectionately during their final photo-call on his retirement after winning a thrilling final race at Ascot, his seventh year of appearing there.

Brown Jack came towards the end of O'Donoghue's career, who was champion flat jockey ten times consecutively between 1914 and 1923. After a slightly mixed start, he came to prominence with The Tetrarch in 1913 when he was already nearly 30 years old. He won the Derby six times, and the Triple Crown twice, something never achieved by any other jockey (see also tribute to him under Sir Gordon Richards, page 80).

THREE OF THE BEST

The three jockeys over the centuries possibly most likely to be considered 'best' are Fred Archer, Sir Gordon Richards and Lester Piggott.

The records of all three men stand up to scrutiny today: Fred Archer rode twenty-one Classic winners and was champion jockey thirteen times. He rode 2,748 winners from 8,084 rides, a strike rate of one win in every 2.9 rides.

By comparison, Sir Gordon Richards, rode 4,870 winners from 21,834 rides, a winning ratio of one in every 4.5 rides; he rode fourteen Classic winners and was champion jockey twenty-six times in his thirty-four-year career.

Lester Piggott, who could reach two meetings in one day thanks to more fixtures and air travel, rode 4,315 winners from 19,552 rides, a ratio, like Sir Gordon, of one win in every 4.5 rides. He won a record twenty-nine Classics, and was champion jockey eleven times in his thirty-seven-year career.

FRED ARCHER

Fred Archer's story is one of the saddest and most poignant in racing. A legendary jockey within his own all too brief lifetime, he was idolised by many but loved only one. Modest and shy off the course, he was ruthless and fired with burning determination to win on it.

He lived and breathed racing, choosing the best horses to ride and people to ride for but when he got out of the train and walked to his Falmouth house in Newmarket it was in to the arms of his beloved wife, Nellie that he fell.

His was the most extraordinary record of that time, the mid- to late 1800s. Bullied to ride regardless of sometimes atrocious conditions by his ambitious father, William, who had won the 1858 Grand National on Little Charley when Fred was a year old, William was determined that his son would be a champion.

Apprenticed to Matt Dawson at Heath House, Newmarket, the 11-year-old Fred was homesick, bullied by the older lads, and in tear-stained letters begged his mother to allow him home.

But slowly it became apparent that he could ride the wayward, recalcitrant and downright rogue horses that others could not. He began to earn the respect of his peers – and to relish his role. A latent burning desire to win began to evolve.

His first race ride, aged 12, was in the Newmarket Town Plate (see page 51), and his first win was in a pony steeplechase at Bangor; he weighed just 4st 11lbs. A year later he won his first flat race, the code for which he is remembered, at Chesterfield. Three years later in 1870, his apprenticeship over, Matt Dawson appointed him the stable's lightweight jockey and he finished second in the overall jockeys' championship.

By 1874, when he was 17 years old, Fred could still ride at the minimum 5st 7lbs and he was champion jockey for the first time with 147 wins. He was to remain champion every year for the rest of his life. But he also shot up in height and weight, meaning that a battle with the scales became his constant companion. He was also appointed stable jockey, riding chiefly for the stable's principal patron, Lord Falmouth; he was to ride twelve Classic winners for him.

Having had to carry 3 or 4st of lead he was now permanently wasting, virtually starving himself, and he invented a devastating purgative known as Archer's mixture.

As his fame grew, men would doff their hats to each other in the street with the words 'Archer's up!' meaning all was well in the world.

He was to ride two of the best horses in the history of horse racing, St Simon and Ormonde, but his greatest achievement was on board Bend Or in the 1880 Derby. He had been savaged a few weeks before on Newmarket Heath by a colt called Muley Edris. He looked beaten as his mount became unbalanced round Tattenham Corner and Robert the Devil had a long lead; but, riding with only one arm, Fred Archer contrived to virtually lift his mount over the line to win by the minimum margin.

In 1881 he won the Derby again, on the American-bred Iroquois. In all he won the Derby five times.

He married his guv'nor's niece, Helen Rose Dawson, known as Nellie, in 1883. His newly built Falmouth House was filled with presents from well-wishers including royalty and crowds lined the streets on their wedding day.

They lost their first child, a son, and for weeks Nellie lay ill. A year later she gave birth to Nellie Rose but, as Fred Archer was dressing in her favourite hunting attire to visit her, Nellie died. He was devastated and never got over the tragedy. He threw himself even more manically to racing and rode a staggering record 246 winners the next season.

But the toll on his health was too great, worsened by his wasting. He caught a fever that turned into typhoid. He was attended in his home by his sister, Mrs Coleman, and eminent physicians, but he was sure he was dying. He distracted Mrs Coleman, and took a revolver from his bedside cabinet. Something made her look round and she grappled with him – but he shot himself. He was 29 years old. Once more the Newmarket streets were lined, but this time in grief for his funeral.

In time, Nelly married and had a son, John Tosetti. In the Second World War he was called up and put on a train, destination unknown – only to find himself marching up Newmarket High Street and billeted in Heath House where his grandfather had been apprenticed.

SIR GORDON RICHARDS

Today the incredible feat of Frankie Dettori's magnificent seven at Ascot's September meeting of 1996, when he went through the card, is well remembered but back in October 1933 the then 29-year-old Gordon Richards did something even more remarkable. Having ridden the winner of the last at Nottingham, he told fellow train passengers en route to Chepstow the next day that he thought he would ride one winner. He scored on all six and then, even more remarkably, he almost repeated the process there the next day. Again, he only fancied one, the odds-on favourite for the last. He was beaten a head and a neck on this – but had ridden the first five before that: twelve consecutive winners.

DID YOU KNOW?

In 2014 Musselburgh and Lingfield racecourses became the first to hold meetings on Good Friday.

The first two English all-weather tracks came about due to many fixtures being lost to bad weather and continually denting the industry's finances. Two artificial tracks were created, the Equitrack at Lingfield Park and a Fibresand track at Southwell, opening within nine days of each other in late 1989. Both tracks also staged all-weather hurdle races until discontinued in 1994.

He ended the season with 259 winners. He beat Fred Archer's record of 246 wins in a season on 8 November. Ironically, this was the anniversary of Archer's death fifty-three years before. In a career that saw him hold a record twenty-six Champion Jockey titles, he beat his own record for wins in a season with 269 in 1943, which stood until the amazing National Hunt jockey Tony 'AP' McCoy notched up 289 wins in the 2001/02 season. As I write, 'AP' has won nineteen National Hunt Jockeys Championships.

Gordon Richards rode a total of 4,870 winners. To date, Tony McCoy has ridden more than 4,000 winners over jumps, arguably an even greater feat given the higher level of injuries in National Hunt racing. One of eight surviving children of a miner in Shropshire, Gordon began his riding career on pit ponies. Work for him began at 7 years old, driving the trap to collect holiday guests from the station; feeding the ponies before school and looking after them again on his return. Home routine also included church three times on Sundays, and sometimes Sunday school as well.

Although there was no racing interest in the family, his small size, 4ft 11½in and affinity with the ponies was to lead him in that direction. But this was only after, at his mother's behest, he had tried being an office clerk after leaving school at 13. Eventually two of the older girls there helped him to answer an advert for a stable hand in a racing stable near Marlborough, Wiltshire. He summoned up courage to tell his parents when he was offered a trial – and he never looked back.

It was New Year's Day 1920, Gordon was 15, and he was leaving home for the first time. It was a quiet train journey from Shropshire to Swindon with his father. His eyes nearly popped out of his head when he was met with a chauffeur-driven car; he had never been in a car before, and he had heard they had the power of twenty horses – could this chauffeur drive one safely, he wondered?

Gordon settled well and loved the new life, which included twelve boys sharing a rat-ridden dormitory and awful food. But he relished the work, the learning, and in time, the riding and in Martin Hartigan he had a boss who became almost like a second father to him.

On Sundays, after riding out at 10.30 a.m. to show the horses to the weekend house guests, they played football, went to church and sometimes had donkey derbies against the female house guests of the stable's proprietor, Jimmy White. The guests were mostly actresses.

The stable jockey was the legendary Steve Donoghue, and Gordon recalls in his memoir *My Story*:

> A tremendous thrill was the first visit of the stable jockey, the great Steve Donoghue … I had thought that he would be very much the famous jockey, and that we apprentices would only catch a glimpse of him in the distance. But that wasn't his way at all.
>
> I was to discover that Steve Donoghue was a lovable, carefree character who just took everything in his stride.
>
> He was immensely popular with everyone and he loved his popularity, for he was a bit of a showman.
>
> … with us he was absolutely genuine, and he had a great natural charm.

... there was no-one quite like Steve on a horse. He had a wonderful action which it was a joy to watch in action.

... We kids were shy and reticent, but that did not last five minutes. He put us all at our ease straightway, by being absolutely natural and simple with all the lads.

When out riding in the string, the young Gordon kept his eyes glued on Donoghue, watching his every move, and his style, and trying to copy him.

At the end of the year, Gordon was given his first race ride, finishing fourth on Clockwork in a big field at Lingfield. His second ride, at Lincoln, came as a reward for kicking the winning penalty in the Sunday football; it was unplaced, but next his gov'nor told him he was to ride Gay Lord in an apprentice race at Leicester.

He had to take the horse there himself, which involved walking him 5 miles to Shrivenham Station and loading him on to the train. From the town station at Leicester he then had to walk him 'three miles of tramlines' to the racecourse.

The head lad told him he thought the horse would win if the trip were further, and in his naivety Gordon took the horse on the wide outside throughout the race, meaning he travelled considerably further than any other horse. Luckily, he still won by an easy 6 lengths.

In his first year as a fully-fledged jockey, 1925, he became champion for the first time with 118 wins. But a few months later he came down with tuberculosis and his embryonic career looked over. However, after only one year out with the debilitating disease he was not only back in the saddle, but was also champion again.

In 1932 he became stable jockey for Fred Darling at the historic Beckhampton stables to the west of Marlborough, Wiltshire.

Flying to meetings was already in vogue in Gordon's day. One day, in 1933 he was flying home from Doncaster, along with his guv'nor Darling, Mrs Hartigan, widow of his first guv'nor, and two others jockeys, F. Lane and Archie Burns.

Richards recalls in his memoir:

I had flown thousands of miles with Dick Pennington, and he was a great pilot. But somehow or other something went wrong that evening. We got off all right; but then we hit the tops of the trees and away we went! Poor Dick was killed and Mrs Hartigan and the Guv'nor were badly cut and had to go to hospital. But, beyond the shaking, none of us jockeys came to any harm.

In June 2000 Frankie Dettori was also involved in a plane crash at Newmarket racecourse, in which the pilot was killed.

The year 1933 was mostly an incredible year for Gordon, with him scoring a record 259 winners and riding those twelve consecutive winners – but he also faced booing that season.

His sensational tally for the season brought many celebrations and congratulations, and recognition well beyond the world of racing. King George V not only sent a telegram, but also gave him a golden cigarette case and two racing pigeons, which formed the foundation pair of a loft he was to keep from then on.

The booing occurred against both jockeys in the two-runner Doncaster Cup. Gordon's horse was doubtful for getting the trip and so he was instructed to stay behind his rival; but the other horse was wayward when leading, and the instructions to its rival was also to stay behind the other horse. The result was a farce, and the time for the 'race' (more like a crawl) was more than seven minutes. Gordon remained convinced of the need for a pacemaker in such a race (as often happens today).

The one thing Gordon retained throughout his career was complete integrity. He was also advised on how to cope with the fame, celebrity status and mixing with royalty and the upper classes in the class-ridden age by an older fellow patient during the year he spent in the sanatorium with TB.

He had one year, however, when all the pressure finally got to him, and it came out in a severe bout of debilitating depression, a secret he successfully guarded at the time.

Gordon rode fourteen Classic winners but for an agonising twenty-eight years the Derby eluded him. Some of the great horses he rode included the temperamental but brilliant filly Sun Chariot, who won the fillies' Triple Crown of 1,000 Guineas, Oaks and St Leger; Gordon believed she could have won the Derby.

Tudor Minstrel won the 1947 2,000 Guineas but was too headstrong in the Derby, fly-jumping and veering right, fighting his able jockey all the way and ruining his chance of staying the trip.

Gordon won the 1,000 and 2,000 Guineas three times each, the Oaks twice and the St Leger five times. In 1942 he won four of the five Classics – but still no Derby.

In 1953 and about to be knighted by the newly-crowned Queen Elizabeth II, he won at last, riding Pinza and, ironically beating the Queen's horse Aureole. In later years he could not decide whether Pinza or Sun Chariot was the best he ever rode and solved it by saying Pinza was the best colt and Sun Chariot the best filly.

The following year, in 1954, he suffered two bad falls and was forced to quit race-riding, and he became a trainer. He died aged 82 in Kintbury, Berkshire, and was buried at St Mary's church, Marlborough; he died on 10 November 1986, exactly 100 years and two days after Fred Archer's death.

COMPARING TWO GREATS FIFTY YEARS APART

Fred Archer and Sir Gordon Richards, two of the greatest flat jockeys, were separated in time by half a century. Fred had to rely on trains and horse-drawn vehicles for transport, but Gordon not only had a chauffeur-driven car, he could also avail of air travel.

In Fred's time there were no starting tapes (let alone stalls), and no draw. He would leave the paddock and make sure he got to the start first and then 'bag' the inside rail. Gordon considered that bad draws cost him many races.

On the other hand, Fred was exceptionally tall for a jockey which meant wasting, virtually starving himself, at the same time as keeping himself in the peak of physical fitness. Gordon was nearly a foot shorter and a natural lightweight, so for him weight was never a problem.

Fred rode in the upright stance of the time, whereas by Gordon's time the forward crouch position had long been adopted.

Writing in his memoir, Gordon said:

I know what it is like to ride more than 200 winners year after year. The planning, the travelling, riding early morning work, the strain on one's nerves is every bit as great as the physical strain of the actual race-riding. You can only survive it successfully if you are well in health and contented in mind. Think of poor Fred Archer, never able to eat normally, wasting away all the time, and subject to all the strains which neither of us could escape, just as severe for the one as the other.

Fred Archer's performance easily outstripped mine and let nobody doubt that. I make this statement with absolute sincerity and certainty. His was an extraordinary, a unique performance ... his achievement in 1885 of riding 246 winners in a season, taking into consideration the difficulties with which he had to contend, is the greatest feat a jockey will ever achieve ... Fred Archer is one of the really great men of the Turf.

Fred Archer's grandson, John Tosetti, told me in the 1980s, 'It is arrant nonsense to compare records because times have changed so much. My grandfather had to ride his hack to reach the races, whereas Gordon Richards would arrive in a chauffeur-driven Rolls, and today's jockeys have helicopters to wing them to two meetings in a day'.

LESTER PIGGOTT

Like Fred Archer, Lester Piggott was tall for a jockey and had to waste hard to do the weight – even though the minimum weight was no longer 5st 7lbs (In 2013 the minimum weight in the UK was raised 2lbs to 8st, the same as in France; Ireland and Australia and the USA already had minimum weights of 8st 4lbs or 8st 7lbs).

Many ordinary men would have conceded victory to the scales, but not Piggott or Archer.

Unlike Archer, Lester had racing coursing through his blood, some two centuries of it going right back to trainer John Day in Hampshire. His son Barnham Day was considered a brilliant trainer. Top jockey Tom Cannon married one of the Day daughters, and their son, Mornington Cannon was champion jockey six times and won six Classics. Kempton Cannon won three Classics soon after the turn of the nineteenth century.

Lester's paternal grandfather, Ernie, won three Grand Nationals: on Jerry M in 1912 and two on Poethyln in 1918 and 1919, and was champion National Hunt jockey three times. Ernie's son Keith, Lester's father, won the 1939 Champion Hurdle on African Sister trained by his uncle, Charlie Piggott. After retiring from the saddle Keith trained Ayala to win the 1963 Grand National.

Lester's maternal grandfather was Frederick Rickaby, who won three Classics and his grandfather, also Frederick, trained the 1855 Derby winner, Wild Dayrell. Fred Junior's son Bill was a jockey, and his sister Iris twice won the only flat race open to female riders at the time, the Newmarket Town Plate. Iris Rickaby married Keith Piggott, and they produced one child, a son they christened Lester Keith.

Lester Piggott rode his first winner at the age of 12 in 1948. Only six years later, at the age of 18, Lester rode his first of a record nine Derby winners, Never Say Die – an appropriate name for this protégé. Yet, as a precocious youngster inclined to ride roughshod over rules and regulations, the young jockey found himself in hot water from the authorities for 'dangerous and erratic riding'. He was banned for six months and, unusually, was barred from his own father's stable for that time.

Throughout his career, communication was not the partially deaf jockey's strong point; he let his riding do the talking.

He rode in the Derby thirty-eight times and won it a record nine times, though his first attempt in 1951, aged just 15, ended at the start when his mount Zucchero refused to start until the rest of the field had gone. Today a rider of either sex has to be 16 before a licence may be granted. (In 2014 Battle Group refused to start for 19-year-old Brendan Powell in the Grand National. After again playing up at the start of the Scottish National the winner of nine races was retired, having fallen out of love with racing.)

Lester was beaten by a neck in the 1952 Derby and then took a slight change of direction when he included some hurdle races in his repertoire: he won twenty hurdle races in two seasons, including the 1954 Triumph Hurdle at Hurst Park on Prince Charlemagne on which a gamble was landed; he had finished unplaced on him in the 1953 Derby. Hurst Park is long since gone under building development, but the race lives on as the 4-year-old Championship at the Cheltenham National Hunt Festival each March.

On Gordon Richards' retirement Lester landed the plum job of stable jockey to Noel Murless. He won the Derby for the first time at the age of 18 in 1954 on Never Say Die, and again on Crepello in 1957. Even so, it was not until he was 24 years old, in 1960, that he first became champion jockey, in which year he won the Derby on St Paddy. He was also champion jockey from 1964–71, and 1981–2.

He left Murless and teamed up, to vintage results, with Ireland's maestro Vincent O'Brien and owner Robert Sangster.

Lester was rejuvenated. In 1968 he won four Classics, and rode Sir Ivor, the horse he still considers his best in spite of the fact that he partnered the brilliant Nijinsky two years later.

Sir Ivor won the 2,000 Guineas and the Derby; that year Lester also won the Irish Derby and the St Leger on Ribero. The third English Classic took him halfway towards Frank Buckle's record of twenty-seven Classics that had stood since 1827.

Two years later, Nijinsky, a highly strung and hugely talented colt won the Triple Crown of 2,000 Guineas, Derby and St Leger; the last horse to do so had been Bahram in 1935, the year Lester was born.

No horse has won the Triple Crown since and only a few have tried, the last being Camelot in 2012; it seemed he only had to turn up to the St Leger to take the Crown, but he finished second.

Lester won the 1972 Derby with Roberto and the St Leger on Boucher; the 1975 Oaks on Juliette Marney (he also rode eight winners at Royal Ascot that year). His seventh Derby came on Empery in 1976, breaking Jem Robinson's record which had stood since 1836. He won the Derby again in 1977 on The Minstrel. He won the Prix de l'Arc de Triomphe twice on Alleged, in 1977 and 1978.

He left Vincent O'Brien in 1980 and joined Henry Cecil, son-in-law of his former boss Noel Murless. He then twice became champion jockey, in 1981 and 1982 when in his late forties.

Part of his ear was torn off in a nasty stalls incident in 1981, yet only one week later he won the 1,000 Guineas on Fairy Footsteps. He also won the Irish Derby on the superb Shergar.

DID YOU KNOW?

In 2014 Musselburgh and Lingfield racecourses became the first to hold meetings on Good Friday.

The first two English all-weather tracks came about due to many fixtures being lost to bad weather and continually denting the industry's finances. Two artificial tracks were created, the Equitrack at Lingfield Park and a Fibresand track at Southwell, opening within nine days of each other in late 1989. Both tracks also staged all-weather hurdle races until discontinued in 1994.

In 1983 Lester scotched rumours of impending retirement and promptly won the Derby again, for the ninth time, on Teenoso. Lester retired – for the first time – at the end of the 1985 flat season and became a trainer at Eve Lodge, Newmarket. In April 2014 this property was put on the market. Lester enjoyed training, with some success, until in 1987 he was jailed for tax evasion.

Remarkably, on his release, he returned to race riding, and just ten days later he won the 1990 Breeders' Cup Mile on Royal Academy. Incredibly, he also won another Classic, on Rodrigo de Triano in the 1992 2,000 Guineas, aged 57, and a number of other top-class races before he finally retired fully in 1995.

Lester won his first race at Haydock Park on The Chase on 18 August 1948 when he was 12 years old. His last win was on the same course, on Palacegate Jack on 5 October 1994, exactly one month short of his 59th birthday. It was his 4,493rd win.

Britain's annual jockeys' awards are known as 'The Lesters' in his honour.

Popularly known as 'The Long Fellow', Lester was unusually tall for a flat jockey and, in his battle to keep his weight down, was reputed to have existed on half a glass of champagne, small coffees and a large cigar each day.

He was also known as the housewives' favourite, as they often put small bets on him, especially in the Derby. Lester won the July Cup on the July Course at Newmarket a record ten times.

Tramore's unusually steep hill and sharp bend came in useful for trainer Liam Browne in 1983, when he had a not unfancied Epsom Derby contender in Carlingford Castle.

Although the Tramore course runs right-handed the trainer realised that if he worked his horse going the other way round it would resemble the world-famous and uniquely difficult Epsom track. He got permission to do a work out on the track – and went on to finish 3 lengths second to Lester Piggott's ninth Derby victor, Teenoso.

MULTIPLE CHAMPION JOCKEYS ON THE FLAT

ELTNATHAN 'NAT' FLATMAN

Elnathan 'Nat' Flatman was the appropriately named first recorded champion jockey on the flat. He won ten Classics and rode for owners that included Lord George Bentinck, Admiral Rous and Lord Derby, among others. He died as the result of an accident in the paddock, aged 50.

1840: 50 winners
1841: 68
1842: 42
1843: 60
1844: 64
1845: 81
1846: 81
1847: 81
1848: 104; the first to reach 100 in a season
1849: 94
1850: 88
1851: 78
1852: 92; 13 consecutive titles

GEORGE FORDHAM

George Fordham weighed only 3st 8lbs and had to use heavy clothing and a big saddle to make his weight up to 5st for his first race ride. He won the Oaks five times but the Derby once from twenty-two attempts. He won his first of fourteen championships at the age of 18 in 1855.

1855: 70
1856: 108
1857: 84
1858: 91
1859: 118
1860: 146
1861: 106
1862: 166
1863: 103; 9 consecutive titles
1865: 142
1867: 143
1868: 110
1869: 95
1871: tied with Charlie Maidment – 86

FRED ARCHER *(see pages 78)*
1874: 147
1875: 172
1876: 207; first to reach 200 in a season

1877: 218
1878: 229
1879: 197
1880: 120
1881: 220
1882: 210
1883: 232
1884: 241
1885: 246
1886: 207; 13 consecutive titles

STEVE DONOGHUE (see page 77)
1914: 129
1915: 62
1916: 43
1917: 42
1918: 66
1919: 129
1920: 143
1921: 141
1922: 102
1923: tied with Charlie Elliott on 89; 10 consecutive titles, including the tie

SIR GORDON RICHARDS (see page 80)
1925: 118
1927: 164
1928: 148
1929: 135
1931: 145
1932: 190
1933: 259
1934: 212
1935: 217
1936: 174
1937: 216
1938: 206
1939: 155

1940: 68; 10 consecutive championships
1942: 67
1943: 65
1944: 88
1945: 104
1946: 212
1947: 269
1948: 224
1949: 261
1950: 201
1951: 227
1952: 231
1953: 191; 12 consecutive championships

LESTER PIGGOTT (see page 86)
1960: 170
1964: 140
1965: 160
1966: 191
1967: 170
1968: 139
1969: 163
1970: 162
1971: 162; 8 consecutive championships
1981: 179
1982: 188
(From 1961 to 1963 the championship was won by Australian Scobie Breasley.)

FRANKIE DETTORI

Although Frankie Dettori has not had as many championships as a number of others he nevertheless is a great tonic for the sport, with his flamboyancy and bubbling enthusiasm. He is also a consummate horseman and jockey, with both flair and empathy.

1994: 233
1995: 211
2004: 192

KIEREN FALLON

Hugely talented and has been retained by a number of the top trainers. He has won 16 Classics including most recently in 2014.

1997: 202
1998: 204
1999: 200
2001: 166
2002: 136
2003: 207

JUMP JOCKEYS

FRED WINTER

My own National Hunt jockey idol was Fred Winter. He was a strong horseman who converted into a top-class trainer (not all successful jockeys do) – and he was an out and out gentleman of integrity and determination.

Fred's father, Fred Senior, was also a jockey who won the Oaks at the age of 16, and Fred himself started on the flat before joining the army in the Parachute Regiment for a while. When he came home it was to National Hunt riding that he turned.

His first win was on his second day of National Hunt racing, but a month later a fall saw him confined to lying flat on his back for three months. When he returned, he teamed up with great success with Captain Ryan Price at Findon; he soon became champion jockey, 1952-3 with a then record of 121 winners, but on the first day of the following season he broke his leg in several places.

The first bet I ever had was 6*d* on Kilmore in the 1962 Grand National, ridden by Fred Winter – and he won.

His best-remembered race was in France in 1962 when, weakened by flu and wasting to do the weight, he rode Mandarin in the French Grand National at Auteuil. Early in the race the horse's bit broke and was left dangling as he galloped on; he also strained a tendon.

Fred, consummate horseman that he was, nevertheless managed to steer him round this complicated course, with some help from French jockeys, to a close-fought victory. Not surprisingly, it is still rated the greatest race ever by many fans.

As a jockey he rode a then-record 923 National Hunt winners before his retirement in 1964. One of the up-and-coming jockeys of that time, Stan Mellor, went on to become the first National Hunt jockey to ride 1,000 winners.

Fred won forty-five times at the Cheltenham National Hunt Festival (seventeen as jockey and twenty-eight as trainer), and is commemorated there by the Fred Winter Juvenile Novices' Handicap Hurdle. He was champion jockey four times and champion trainer eight times.

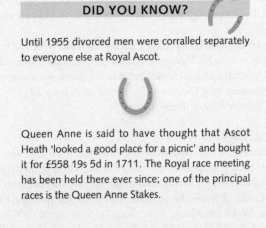

DID YOU KNOW?

Until 1955 divorced men were corralled separately to everyone else at Royal Ascot.

Queen Anne is said to have thought that Ascot Heath 'looked a good place for a picnic' and bought it for £558 19s 5d in 1711. The Royal race meeting has been held there ever since; one of the principal races is the Queen Anne Stakes.

He won the Grand National twice, on Sundew in 1957, and Kilmore in 1962. He then trained two Grand National winners, Jay Trump in 1965 and Anglo in 1966. Jay Trump arrived from America where he had already twice won the Maryland Hunt Cup (he was to win it again on his return) and was Fred's first runner as a trainer.

He won the Cheltenham Gold Cup on Saffron Tartan in 1961 and Mandarin in 1962, and he trained Midnight Court to win it in 1978 when the race was postponed to April following snow on Gold Cup day at the festival in March.

Bula won two Champion Hurdles (1971-2) for him as a trainer, as did Lanzarote in 1974 and Celtic Shot in his retirement year, 1988. He rode three winners of it himself: Clair Soleil in 1955, Fare Time in 1959 and Eborneezer in 1961.

Crisp was his Champion Chase winner in 1971 (Queen Mother Champion Chase since 1980, in honour of that great lady and National Hunt fan's 80th birthday) two years before his epic attempt at Aintree.

He rode Halloween to victory in the King George VI chase in 1952 and 1954, and Saffron Tartan in 1960, and he trained Pendil to win it in 1972 and 1973.

But Fred was about much more than wins and statistics. He was always willing to have a word with people and to listen (though his lads might not have agreed with that in the early mornings).

To hear him quietly speaking about each horse of the string as it came by him at his Uplands, Lambourn, stables was a privilege. He was a master of his chosen art. He went out on a winner with his last runner, Stag Dinner at Stratford on 4 June 1988.

Fred Winter died in 2004, aged 77.

CRISP AND RED RUM

Fred Winter trained probably the best horse to lose the Grand National in the magnificent chaser Crisp. The big, nearly black, horse had carried all before him in his native Australia, so he was sent to England where he won his initial handicap chase carrying 12st 7lbs by 15 lengths.

He won the 1971 Two Mile Champion Chase but the following year failed to stay the Gold Cup distance; and yet, in 1973, he contested the marathon Grand National. And how nearly he won it! He carried joint top weight of 12st yet jumped his way to the front and by the end of the first circuit was leading by at least 20 lengths. How he loved those big fences! Each time he saw the next one looming he gathered more pace and soared over, giving Richard Pitman a dream ride and galloping further and further ahead of his rivals.

Just one horse began to break away from the remainder in pursuit, and as Crisp finally tired on that long, long run in this other horse, carrying only 10st 5lbs, wore him down and caught Crisp in the shadow of the post.

And the name of that horse? Red Rum, who went on to prove himself the greatest Grand National horse of all time. Trained by Ginger McCain from a garage in Southport, with the sand beach his gallops, Red Rum won again the next year when he carried 12st.

He finished runner-up to duel Cheltenham Gold Cup winner L'Escargot in 1975 and to Rag Trade in 1976, but in 1977, at the age of 12, Red Rum quite incredibly won again. He was a true course specialist with the agility of a cat and an ability to avoid trouble.

His first ever win had been a dead-heat on the flat at, of all places, Aintree (which has long since ceased flat racing). Apart from his Grand National wins, he also won the Scottish National in 1974, shortly after winning the Aintree showpiece. He carried 11st 13lbs – not far off emulating the mighty Arkle who carried 12st 7lbs – to victory in the Irish Grand National shortly after winning his first Cheltenham Gold Cup.

Today, Ginger's son, Donald, has become a leading UK trainer from the stunning stables at Bankhouse, set in 200 acres at Cholmondeley Castle Estate, Cheshire.

Ginger won a fourth Grand National with Amberleigh House in 2004, and Donald trained the winner of the 2011 race in Ballabriggs.

JOHN FRANCOME

The sheer artistry of John Francome in the saddle remains a highlight for anyone who loves National Hunt racing. He could have had no better grounding than with Fred Winter and as trainer and jockey they won many of the top races. John rode a total of 1,138 winners, and was champion jockey seven times between 1976 and 1985.

After he retired from the saddle John spent a short time training in Lambourn and then became a novelist and TV racing presenter, something which suited his cheerful yet thoughtful and knowledgeable style. Today, he has taken over as president of the Injured Jockeys Fund following the death of the founder, Lord Oaksey, a cause for which he is enthusiastic and eminently suitable.

RICHARD DUNWOODY

Richard Dunwoody began his career as an amateur and was champion jockey for three successive years from 1992/93 to 1994/95. He is best remembered for his association with the much-loved grey Desert Orchid, who won an incredible thirty-four times, and made the King George VI Chase his own at Kempton on Boxing Day, winning it four times. Desert Orchid also won the 1989 Cheltenham Gold Cup in heavy ground conditions.

It seemed unlikely that any horse would emulate Desert Orchid at Kempton, yet Kauto Star won the prestigious chase five times, as well as two Cheltenham Gold Cups.

PETER SCUDAMORE

Peter Scudamore, whose father Michael won the 1959 Grand National on Oxo, won the National Hunt jockeys championship ten consecutive times from 1985/86 to 1994/95; in addition, he tied with John Francome in 1981/82. He broke the 200 mark with 221 in 1988/89. Michael Scudamore died in the summer of 2014.

RICHARD JOHNSON

Spare a thought for National Hunt jockey Richard (Dickie) Johnson. He is not only one of an elite band to have ridden a thousand winners, he has actually ridden more than 2,500 winners – yet he has never been champion jockey. Why? Because he joined the senior jockeys' ranks the year after one Tony (AP) McCoy first won the championship, a title he has held for nineteen consecutive years (to the end of the 2013-14 season), amassing a staggering 4,000-plus winners in the process.

The start of Richard Johnson's career was oh so similar to Tony McCoy's: at 18 years of age, in 1995, he was Conditional Jockeys Champion. Thereafter, he was destined to fill the runner-up's shoes (once he was third in the table with Timmy Murphy sneaking second), but none of the good, senior jockeys have been able to oust 'AP' from top spot, even in years when he has spent time sidelined with injury.

Almost throughout his career Dickie Johnson has been retained by trainer Philip Hobbs in Somerset, an enduring and loyal association.

Interestingly, given they are the two most successful National Hunt jockeys of the late 1990s-2000s, it took Tony McCoy fifteen attempts at the Grand National before he won it (on Don't Push It in 2010), and so far Dickie Johnson is still counting his attempts. He finished second twice, most recently in 2014 on Balthazar King.

Dickie Johnson, one-time boyfriend of Zara Phillips, daughter of Princess Anne, rode his 1,000th winner at Stratford in 2003, aboard a horse called Quedex. He was the eighth National Hunt jockey to do so, after Stan Mellor, John Francome, Peter Scudamore, Richard Dunwoody, Adrian Maguire, Peter Niven and Tony McCoy.

He rode his 2,000th winner at Newbury in December 2009, on a horse named Fighting Chance, an ironic name given his efforts at winning the jockeys' championship. He became the first jockey to ride the big four races at the National Hunt Festival, Cheltenham, on Anzum in the 1999 Stayers (now World) Hurdle; the Gold Cup in 2000 aboard Looks Like Trouble; the 2002 Queen Mother Champion Chase on Flagship Uberalles, and the Champion Hurdle on Rooster Booster in 2003. Since then this feat has been matched by Barry Geraghty and Ruby Walsh.

Richard Johnson's 2,500-plus winners is more than double that of any other National Hunt jockey, bar AP.

TONY 'AP' McCOY

Monday 9 February 2009, Plumpton, set beneath the South Downs in Sussex remains one of my highlights in racing, even though I wasn't there and watched it on television.

Plumpton is a 'minor' track whose meetings are most often on a quiet Monday (as this one was). Tony McCoy had been stuck on 2,998 winners for ten days but he had a good book of rides here. But the meeting remained in doubt because of rain. A number of recent meetings had been cancelled through waterlogging and this one only just managed to pass an inspection.

Could the landmark be achieved here? Enthusiasts flocked to the little course. Tony, who has won far and away more National Hunt races than any other rider in the history of the sport, was poised for his 3,000th win. The press had been following him around with even more interest than usual over the last week, just as they had back in 1971 when Stan Mellor came up with the first ever 1,000 National Hunt wins on a quiet Tuesday at Nottingham; he had travelled to Cheltenham more than a week earlier on 999.

Tony needed two more wins. The first came in vintage McCoy style. He rode his next mount hard at the last fence as only he can, and the horse took a horrendous looking fall, spiralling Tony into the turf. This is the danger that jump jockeys take every day. His bid for his 3,000th winner could have ended there and then. For a moment it looked as if it had, but the man appears to be made of India rubber and up he, well, not quite bounced but was fit enough to ride Restless D'Artaix – and galloped first past the post and into the record books.

Plumpton was where I had been to Pony Club camp as a child and where I had competed in a race on foot – and dreamed of riding up the slope by the stands and stables, left-handed round the narrow oval top and sweeping down the far side hill towards the little railway station before heading back up to the stands and

DID YOU KNOW?

Women were not allowed to ride under the Rules of Racing, Flat or NH, in Great Britain until 1972, when a limited number of ladies' Flat races were introduced. Women had to wait until January of 1976 before they could ride in steeplechases or hurdle races.

In 1962 the Jockey Club made chin straps compulsory for women, but not for men, in point-to-points 'because of their extra hair'. They become compulsory for all two years later.

the finishing post. Little could I have dreamed of watching this momentous piece of racing history there.

Only four and a half short years later, on 7 November 2013, this incredibly dedicated man notched up his 4,000th winner on Mountain Tunes at Towcester, a wide open course with a stiff uphill climb to the post that is set within the Northamptonshire market town. For the last while he had been riding only horses for the owner who retained him, the legendary Irishman JP McManus, so that he could mark this landmark in his famous green and gold colours.

He did it in his own inimitable style, for he looked beaten. But you never give up hope with a McCoy-ridden horse until the post has passed because McCoy never gives up. Time and again he will conjure victory from a seemingly impossible position.

A bit like Gordon Richards in his quest to ride a Derby winner, for AP it sometimes seemed as if the Grand National just wouldn't come his way. Gordon won the Derby at the end of his long career, and in 2010, AP finally won the Grand National at the fifteenth time of asking.

Later that year he deservedly became the first jockey recipient of the BBC's Sports Personality of the Year.

Ulster-born Anthony McCoy was apprenticed to one of Ireland's great flat race trainers, Jim Bolger. He won his first race for him in 1992, aged 17.

But jumping was to be Tony's game. He moved to England as a conditional jockey for leading National Hunt trainer Toby Balding in Hampshire, a clever mentor with young jockeys, a good trainer and first-class administrator.

That first year, 1994-5, AP McCoy was champion conditional jockey with a record seventy-four winners. His future clearly lay with a bigger stable and he moved to Martin Pipe in Somerset and became champion jockey, a position he has retained every year since. At the end of the 2013-14 season, he has taken it to nineteen years consecutively. The longest sequence previously for a National Hunt champion jockey was the seven of Peter Scudamore.

Tony McCoy was retained by the all-conquering innovative training maestro Martin Pipe for seven years. It seemed an unstoppable partnership, but in 2004 he was lured, reportedly, by a retainer of £1 million per year. McCoy teamed up with leading Irish owner J.P. McManus who had installed another Irish hero,

Jonjo O'Neill as trainer in Jackdaws Castle in the Cotswolds not far from Cheltenham. Jonjo will forever be remembered for his momentous Gold Cup win on the mare, Dawn Run, when having relinquished the lead and was seemingly beaten coming into the last fence.

Tony McCoy has won the Cheltenham Gold Cup on Mr Mulligan and Synchronised; the Champion Hurdle on Make A Stand, Brave Inca and Binocular; the Queen Mother Champion Chase on Edredon Bleu; and King George VI Chase, Kempton Park's annual Boxing Day showpiece, on Best Mate.

Gordon Richards is, at the time of writing, the only jockey to have been knighted. For the impeccably well-mannered Tony McCoy, awarded MBE in 2003 and OBE in 2010, his moment will surely come. No sportsman deserves it more.

Season	Jockey	Status	Wins
2013–14	A.P. McCoy	Professional	218
2012–13	A.P. McCoy	Professional	185
2011–12	A.P. McCoy	Professional	199
2010–11	A.P. McCoy	Professional	218
2009–10	A.P. McCoy	Professional	195
2008–09	A.P. McCoy	Professional	186
2007–08	A.P. McCoy	Professional	140
2006–07	A.P. McCoy	Professional	184
2005–06	A.P. McCoy	Professional	178
2004–05	A.P. McCoy	Professional	200
2003–04	A.P. McCoy	Professional	209
2002–03	A.P. McCoy	Professional	258
2001–02	A.P. McCoy	Professional	289
2000–01	A.P. McCoy	Professional	191
1999–2000	A.P. McCoy	Professional	245
1998–99	A.P. McCoy	Professional	186
1997–98	A.P. McCoy	Professional	253
1996–97	A.P. McCoy	Professional	190
1995–96	A.P. McCoy	Professional	175
1994–95	Richard Dunwoody	Professional	160
1993–94	Richard Dunwoody	Professional	197
1992–93	Richard Dunwoody	Professional	173
1991–92	Peter Scudamore	Professional	175
1990–91	Peter Scudamore	Professional	141

1989–90	Peter Scudamore	Professional	170
1988–89	Peter Scudamore	Professional	221
1987–88	Peter Scudamore	Professional	132
1986–87	Peter Scudamore	Professional	123
1985–86	Peter Scudamore	Professional	91
1984–85	John Francome	Professional	101
1983–84	John Francome	Professional	131
1982–83	John Francome	Professional	106
1981–82	John Francome/		
	Peter Scudamore	Professional	120
1957–58	Fred Winter	Professional	82
1956–57	Fred Winter	Professional	80
1955–56	Fred Winter	Professional	74
1954–55	Tim Molony	Professional	67
1953–54	Dick Francis	Professional	76
	Fred Winter	Professional	121
1951–52	Tim Molony	Professional	99
1950–51	Tim Molony	Professional	83
1949–50	Tim Molony	Professional	95
1948–49	Tim Molony	Professional	60
1940–41	Gerry Wilson	Professional	22
1939–40	Fred Rimell	Professional	24
1938–39	Fred Rimell	Professional	61
1937–38	Gerry Wilson	Professional	59
1936–37	Gerry Wilson	Professional	45
1935–36	Gerry Wilson	Professional	57
1934–35	Gerry Wilson	Professional	73
1933–34	Gerry Wilson	Professional	56
1932–33	Gerry Wilson	Professional	61
1931–32	Billy Stott	Professional	77
1930–31	Billy Stott	Professional	81
1929–30	Billy Stott	Professional	77
1928–29	Billy Stott	Professional	76
1927–28	Billy Stott	Professional	88
1915*	Ernie Piggott	Professional	44
1914*	Jack Anthony	Amateur	60
1913*	Ernie Piggott	Professional	60
1912*	Ivor Anthony	Professional	78
1911*	W. Payne	Professional	76
1910*	Ernie Piggott	Professional	67

1909*	R. Gordon	Professional	45
1908*	P. Cowley	Professional	65
1907*	Frank Mason	Professional	59
1906*	Frank Mason	Professional	58
1905*	Frank Mason	Professional	73
1904*	Frank Mason	Professional	59
1903*	Percy Woodland	Professional	54
1902*	Frank Mason	Professional	67
1901*	Frank Mason	Professional	58
1900*	H.S. Sidney	Amateur	53

* calendar year rather than campaign season.

9

RACING TERMINOLOGY

BLACKSMITH/FARRIER

There is an old saying, 'no foot, no horse'. True, I'm afraid. The blacksmith is someone you mustn't stint on, even when your horse is on holiday and not wearing shoes, for every six to eight weeks his feet will need trimming; this is much like paring your own finger nails. If a horse's feet are left to grow too long, he will start putting all his weight on his heels, because his toenails are too long for him to balance on – in extreme cases they will curl right over at the front like a clown's shoe, and this will cause severe lameness.

Your blacksmith will be a good friend and will be able to correct certain foot faults through remedial shoeing. Also, if your horse is lame and you cannot see an obvious reason, it may well be worth asking your blacksmith to visit before calling the vet. Racehorses are often fitted with aluminium shoes especially for racing because they are very light.

BLANKET

A rug to keep a horse warm in the winter. Racehorses are among the best looked after of any animal; in the winter their coat will be clipped so that they don't sweat too much when galloping, then when he is at rest he is kept well rugged up. These days there are marvellous thermal products on the market; equally, an old duvet tucked under a lighter rug and buckled securely will keep him warm.

A 'blanket finish' describes the end of a race in which several horses are so close together that metaphorically they could all be covered by one blanket.

BLOW OUT

This doesn't refer to too much food, or to a tyre puncturing, but is an expression used when doing up the girth of a saddle. Very often a horse will 'blow out', literally expanding its stomach in reaction to the girthing. It can result in a very quick fall and embarrassment if the girth has not been tightened a second time before mounting.

A blow out also means a short, sharp piece of work to clear a horse's wind.

BOLT

The bolt on a stable door; there are a number of different types, some being necessary to keep in the Houdini type of animal who can pull back a conventional bolt with his teeth.

'It's no good locking the stable door after the horse has bolted' – too late to do something about it then.

To bolt: a runaway horse. The word bolt originates from the name given to a short, thick arrow with a blunt head, so, 'the horse bolted' – 'shot off like an arrow'. One of the most frightening experiences for a rider, and one it is hoped he will never have to cope with. It takes a very brave person to 'bail out' from a bolting horse but there are a few occasions when it may be the lesser of two evils.

To bolt in, or bolt up: when a racehorse wins a race very easily.

When a racehorse has 'shot its bolt' in a race it has run out of either stamina or wind, or both, and, try as it might, it cannot do enough to win.

BOOTS

No, not green wellies, or these days highly colourful and fashion-able ones, but the 'boots' applied to many racehorses particularly in jump races. Either put on all four lower legs or the front two or hind pair, they offer protection from minor birch injuries or over-reaches.

The boots are usually fastened with Velcro. What on earth did we do before Velcro? Well, in the case of horse boots, we fastened about ten tiny buckles and tucked the ends into tight fitting 'keepers' on each boot, made of leather that had to be oiled regularly; it was all very time-consuming, unlike the quick wipe down of today's synthetic material and Velcro fastening.

BOX

Either the stable in which a horse lives, or the vehicle in which it is transported.

BREAST PLATE

A breast plate goes around the chest of a racehorse and attaches to the girth; it prevents the saddle from slipping back.

BRIDLE

Nothing to do with either a bride, or with taking exception to or being resentful of something or someone. The bridle is the headwear used to control and guide a horse, complete with a bit in his mouth. In Greek mythology it is said to have been invented by Pelethronius. A bridle is probably more important than a saddle to ride a horse but Mandarin managed to win in Paris with the bit dangling out of his mouth. And I remember a point-to-point at Parham in Sussex when the winner, a chestnut mare called Pervola, had lost her whole bridle during the race, yet her amateur rider managed to steer her to success.

BROKEN WIND

See Gone in the Wind.

BUMPERS

National Hunt flat races are known as bumpers. The term is a derogatory one for amateur riders who bumped up and down in the saddle. Today, most professional jockeys bump in the saddle when a horse comes off the bit (is tiring); the jockey then 'bumps him along.' The difference is probably that professionals and good amateurs do it in a rhythmic way and therefore do not unbalance their horse.

The idea of National Hunt flat races is to give a young National Hunt-bred horse racecourse experience without being faced with obstacles, or with taking on speedier, earlier maturing flat horses, before it goes hurdling or chasing.

CANNON

Nothing to do with guns, but the equivalent of the shin-bone between the knee and fetlock (the joint just above the hoof) of a horse. On the hind leg it is known as the shank.

CANTER

The term is said to have been invented by pilgrims in the Middle Ages riding from London along the North Downs to the place where Thomas á Becket was murdered in Canterbury Cathedral. They discovered a three-time gait that was more comfortable than a trot and slower, and therefore less arduous for the horse, than a full gallop. They called it a Canterbury pace; it became known as 'cantering gallop' and has long since been contracted to 'canter'.

To 'win in a canter' is when a horse wins so easily that he hardly needs to gallop at the end of the race and can still win easily.

CHANGING THE WHIP

Not replacing one whip with another, but a jockey pulling the whip through from one hand to the other.

CHESTNUT

A horse's coat that is nearly orange in colour. Horses also grow a 'chestnut' on the insides of their hocks (the joint halfway down a horse's hind legs) and inside and slightly above the knees on their front legs; it is a horny growth and will fall off and re-grow; dogs will enjoy chewing it like a bone, as they also do for hoof trimmings after the farrier has pared a horse's feet.

'That old chestnut' applies to anyone telling an over-used, stale story or joke, and I'm sure it can apply to racehorse owners as much as golfers and fishermen.

CLENCH

Nothing to do with a fist or your teeth, but the term for the nail with which the horse's shoe is held in place. One of the first signs that a horse needs a new set of shoes is that the clenches 'rise', causing the shoe to become loose.

COLIC

Not dissimilar to your baby's wind, but potentially far more serious. If the horse keeps throwing his head round to his sides, is sweating for no apparent reason, and appears restless phone the vet immediately. Don't try to cope on your own. Colic is exceedingly painful to the animal and unfortunately does sometimes result in death. Very often a post mortem will show that he has twisted his gut, making death inevitable.

COLT

The term for an unneutered young male horse, up to three years. After that he is a 'full horse' or, if he is lucky enough to stand at stud, a stallion. Once he has been neutered (gelded/castrated), he is a gelding. Thoroughbreds that are bred to be National Hunt (jumping) horses are usually gelded as yearlings; flat race horses mainly race as colts; they may then be gelded if either they have not been successful and cannot then commercially be used at stud; or if they become a bit 'leary', and gelding gets them back on the straight and narrow.

COLOURS

Of racehorses: bay, brown, black, chestnut, grey. Other colours – roan, palomino, cream, albino, dun, skewbald, piebald, appaloosa – are found in non-thoroughbreds or 'common' horses. However, many grey horses are born a different colour, often chestnut, and as its mature coat is coming through he may well appear roan in colour (that is, an admixture of hair colour).

The most usual colour for a racehorse is bay. A bay is a brown horse but with a black mane and tail which differentiates it from a brown horse, which is brown all over. A black horse is nearly always really a dark brown, though just occasionally there is a true black. There is a saying that owners don't like to register a horse as black, as that was the colour chosen for pulling a hearse, and they associated that with bad luck in races. A bay horse comes in varying shades, from a bright bay (mahogany) to a light bay (nearly as light as pine wood) to a dark bay that is very similar to a brown. The distinguishing feature is the black 'points', i.e. lower limbs, and the black mane and tail.

Probably the nearest colour to best describe chestnut is orange. There can be a light chestnut, or one so pale that it is known as 'wishy washy', or a liver chestnut that is much darker in colour, nearly like a bay except that he has a chestnut mane and tail, whereas the bay, as we have seen, has a black mane and tail. There can also be 'red' chestnut.

Chestnut mares gained a reputation for hot-headedness over the years, but find a good one and, like the little girl with a curl in the middle of her forehead, when she is good, she is very, very good.

When you see a horse that looks white, he is a grey. Don't ask me why! Tradition again, no doubt. There are varying shades of grey and very often they go with a horse's age: as a foal he may be an iron or steel grey, with so many black hairs mixed in that from afar he will look nearly black. In middle-age he may become a flea-bitten grey, that is a grey covered in little brown spots, and in old age he will look white, but the nearest we can get to calling him that is white grey. Interestingly, as a grey horse changes its colour through its life, the black pigment that disappears may accumulate in lumps, often behind the ear or under the throat or belly; these lumps are benign and harmless though not very sightly! One parent is likely to have been grey. All grey horses originate from the Alcock Arabian, one of the early imported stallions.

COLOURS OR SILKS

The design of the jacket worn by the jockey. To some people one of the great joys of ownership is watching a horse race in their own personally chosen colours. Every set of colours is unique to the owner to whom they are registered by the governing horse racing body, and they make up a key image of horse racing; the great kaleidoscope of twenty or more horses and jockeys skimming over a flight in the hurly burly of a big novice hurdle race.

Flat race jockeys wear lightweight colours made of silk (known as silks); National Hunt jockeys, who generally ride at a heavier weight, used to wear colours knitted in wool (welcome in the winter weather prevalent in this sport) but increasingly these, too, are made of silk (or nylon, or another equally lightweight synthetic material).

Usually there is one main body colour, and then to distinguish it from other owners' colours, there will usually be a feature in another colour, such as a sash, cross-belt, checks, quarters, star or disc. The arms will usually have the main basic colour, but there may be hoops, spots or stars on these. The cap may be of a totally different colour, or it may follow the main body theme with quarters, hoops and so on. The days when pictures or other fancy imagery could be on the main body have gone, but one or two survive, notably Raymond Keogh's red stag's head on white, representing his love of Ireland's Ward Union Staghounds.

COW HOCKS

You don't want a racehorse with these, he might not be able to run very fast; they resemble a bow-legged man. The hock is the joint halfway down a horse's hind leg, and which propels a horse across the ground or over a jump. Cow hocks turn inwards, which is a conformation fault.

DANDY BRUSH

Nothing foppish about this one ... a simple, firm-bristled brush for grooming a horse with, though it may be too firm for a thin skinned thoroughbred and a softer body brush is better.

DERBY

The most famous Classic race run over 1½ miles of the challenging, undulating course at Epsom for 3-year-old thoroughbreds. Its name was decided by the toss of a coin between its cofounders, the Earl of Derby and Sir Charles Bunbury in 1780. Derby won the honour of the name but to Bunbury went the accolade of winning the first Derby, with his colt Diomed.

The race spawned many imitations, notably in 1785 the Kentucky Derby, the first leg of the American Triple Crown, and the Hickstead Derby in show-jumping (founded by the late

Douglas Bunn on his Sussex course in 1961). Imagine if local entertainment now included a Donkey Bunbury ...

DISH

Nothing to do with cooking or crockery, this is where a horse throws one or both of its front legs sideways, instead of straight in front of it. It is a conformation fault, yet many horses will win races with it (they just won't win in the show-ring).

DR GREEN

A euphemism for grass, the greatest tonic of all. Horses are 'turned out to grass' for their holidays.

EWE NECK

Where the horse's neck is 'upside down', i.e. concave instead of convex.

GELDING

See Colt.

GONE IN THE WIND

Not with the wind; a general term for breathing defects. A horse that is broken winded, a roarer or a whistler will make a considerable noise when cantering, let alone galloping. A hobday or tie-back operation may cure the problem. Increasingly, racehorses have operations for comparatively minor wind defects and often win on their next racing appearance.

HANDICAP

Not a disability but an allocation of weights to be carried by each horse in a race, designed to give all horses an equal chance; in theory, they should finish in line abreast. The most famous handicap race is probably the Grand National at Aintree, and on the flat, the Lincoln at the beginning of the season; the Ebor at

York in August, and the Cambridgeshire and Cesarewitch make up the autumn double at the end.

Races like the Classics on the flat and, in jumping, the Cheltenham Gold Cup and Champion Hurdle are run on a 'level playing field' off the same weights (bar an allowance for mares/ fillies) and so, in theory at least, the best horse will win.

JARRED

Nothing to do with drinking; a horse's legs may become jarred, i.e. tender or sore, if run on ground that is too firm for him.

LEG

Don't be too surprised when you hear someone referring to his horse as 'having a leg'. Well, yes, four of them, you might think innocently. But 'having a leg' is horse-speak for lameness, usually tendon trouble. And when they are pulled or strained, a horse's tendons, like an athlete's sinews, will be swollen, inflamed and painful, and will take a long time to repair. After initial poulticing, cold hosing and bandaging, time is the principal healer.

Pulling a tendon can be the result of bad luck, putting a foot in a rabbit hole, for instance, but is usually caused by fast galloping. The horse will be more susceptible if it is not sufficiently fit; racehorses are particularly prone to it. The sinews literally 'break down' under the strain. Recovery may be three months, six months or a year, depending on the severity of the damage.

MAIDEN

A maiden race is nothing to do with females, but is a race for a horse of either sex that has not as yet won a race.

MAKING A NOISE

See Gone in the Wind (not *Gone with the Wind*).

MONKEY

A betting term for £500. A horse can also be 'a bit of a monkey', i.e. wayward. The term monkey on a stick comes from the American Tod Sloan (see page 74) who at the turn of the nineteenth century was ridiculed and called a 'monkey on a stick' because he crouched forward over the horse's neck. The style offers less wind resistance and therefore assists the horse in running faster and in time it became universally adopted.

PACEMAKER

A horse put in a race by a trainer to set the pace for his other better fancied horse, to ensure a true run race (see Sir Gordon Richards, page 80).

PULLED UP

As in 'pulled up three out'. A jockey will usually pull up a horse, that is, slow him to a walk thereby putting him out of the race, when all chance of victory has gone, and especially if the horse is either unfit or else hasn't the stamina for the race distance; if he has made a bad mistake at a fence and lost his chance; or if the jockey feels him go lame. The 'three out' refers to how many fences were left to jump at the time he was pulled up.

READING THE RACECARD

For a newcomer the racecard can appear to be little more than hieroglyphics – OK, it's fairly obvious what the horses' names are (pronouncing them may be a different matter); the names of the owner, trainer and jockey are clear, and there is usually a graphic showing the colours the jockey will be wearing.

But there are many abbreviations.

So, you see a horse's name with the initials BF beside it. This is not what you (probably) think it means: it is short for 'Beaten Favourite', meaning that it failed to win in spite of starting favourite last time it ran. On the other hand, CD beside a horse's name means it has won not only on this very course, but also over the same distance as today's race; a mighty good tip, one would hope.

If you read f14 this means that in its last three races the horse fell, won, and was fourth. Ch f stands for chestnut filly; bg for bay gelding; c stands for colt, and m for mare; ur means unseated rider, su slipped up, r refused. The card is likely also to give a short summary of the horse's chances in a given race; form notes of its previous runs below that will give its price, its official rating, jockey, the weight it carried, and where it finished, e.g: won 9L 4L from xx and xx; so he finished 9 lengths ahead of the second horse, who was himself 4 lengths ahead of the third. The guide then gives an abbreviation of the course, PUN meaning Punchestown, followed by the date, the number of runners (7rn), the type of race, (nov.hdl is short for novice hurdle), and what the going was like, e.g. Gd/Yld is good to yielding.

The figure under the horse's name gives its year of birth, followed by 'by Bob Back (USA) – Mrs Marples', showing that the horse was by the sire Bob Back who was himself born in America, and out of a dam called Mrs Marples.

Sometimes the horse's name will be chosen from the names of the sire and dam, for example Hidden Cyclone is by Stowaway (GB) out of Hurricane Debbie. It can be fun for the breeder or future owner choosing such names; my mother bred a horse called Spider Man, who was by Manicou out of Tangled Web. Tangled Web was by Tangle out of Royal Catch. There is a thirty-year rule on names, and unless a horse has been very famous, such as Arkle or Desert Orchid, or the winner of certain top world races, the name becomes available again for registration. Hence, as I write there is another Tangled Web, trained by Charlie Swan and owned by Ireland's leading owner JP McManus – the breeding appears to have nothing to do with the name, but it has done rather better on the racecourse with two wins and two seconds from six runs to date, and that is far more important.

RIG

Nothing to do with oil, nor with dressing well, a rig is neither a full horse, nor a gelding; it occasionally happens when one testicle has not come down sufficiently for castration and the poor animal ends up neither one thing nor another, leaving him frustrated and sometimes difficult to handle.

TO RIG A RACE

To swindle, to act fraudulently, to rig the betting market – all strictly against the rules, of course, and with modern-day policing by racing authorities, increasingly difficult for anyone to achieve. One of the reasons for racing's popularity these days is its inherent integrity.

SELLER

The lowest class of race in the UK in which the winner is put up for auction immediately after the race; they are not held in Ireland.

SOCKS/STOCKINGS

The white hair that often grows on the lower legs of an otherwise bay, brown or chestnut horse; socks will be short, just above the foot, stockings may go all the way up to the knee.

TO BACK

To mount a horse for the first time when breaking it. Also, to bet on (back) a horse in a race.

WEED

Something in the garden or a spindly, puny, pathetic-looking horse, usually thoroughbred.

WITHER

Not a withering look when your horse fails, but the point between a horse's neck and its back, and from which its height is measured.

10

RACEHORSE
TRANSPORT THROUGH
THE AGES

BY AIR

Vincent O'Brien, master trainer from County Tipperary, Ireland, was the first trainer ever to fly horses across the Irish Sea to race at Cheltenham. The usual mode of transport was by ferry and lorry. O'Brien had won the 1948 Cheltenham Gold Cup with Cottage Rake. The following year he took the unprecedented step of taking three horses to Cheltenham and flying them over. It was unheard of.

Vincent O'Brien hired a former RAF transport plane and they flew from Shannon; after about 20 minutes Cottage Rake 'went mad', and on landing 'there was great rejoicing and swigs of whiskey when they landed safely' according to the lads, as recorded in *Vincent O'Brien: The Official Biography*.

All three horses won.

Cottage Rake took the middle of his three Gold Cups, Hatton's Grace the first of his three Champion Hurdles, and Castledermot won the 4-mile National Hunt Chase for amateur riders.

In the 1960s Arkle used to travel by plane to run in England. His lad Johnny Lumley, recalls: 'It was the early days of flying horses and the planes were adapted cargo vessels. They were quite dangerous and very cold. The stalls were rough and ready with sharp edges, and when we landed people had to go around looking for a ramp to bring the horses down.'

He adds: 'It was freezing cold and we couldn't talk because it was so noisy so we used to sit on a bale of straw and play cards.'

The flight from Birmingham to Dublin took two and a half hours. That was in the days when it was customary for a stallion to cover forty mares a season. Nowadays these globe-trotting super-studs complete a full northern hemisphere of possibly 200 mares – and then travel by jet plane to the southern hemisphere, probably Australia, to mate with a similar number, in other words ten times the old norm.

Massive numbers would be possible by AI (artificial insemination) but while that is allowed with, say, show-jumpers, it is not for thoroughbreds. This is partly so that every mating may be witnessed live to eliminate any dubiety (although today DNA testing would see to that), but it also prevents over-breeding – and also ensures that high prices for the most sought-after progeny are maintained.

Sometimes a single horse competing in a major event abroad will be accompanied by as many as five individual minders: two lads, two security men and a blacksmith.

BY WATER

Until the advent of flight, horses had nevertheless travelled abroad for many centuries, by boat. William the Conqueror had all his men's horses brought across the English Channel by boat. The first three progenitors of the thoroughbred, the Byerley Turk, and the Godolphin and Darley Arabians will have come the same way, to improve the racehorses of England beyond recognition in the late seventeenth and early eighteenth century.

From the end of the nineteenth century horses were conveyed by special freight vessels between Folkestone, Kent, and Boulogne in France. They were lifted on to the ferry in crates, put in stalls, and lifted out the other end.

A journey to Australia would mean that a horse had no exercise at all for six weeks; they were fed, hayed, watered and mucked out, but they didn't leave the confines of their stall – although in 1932 a treadmill was supplied to keep the Dutch horses semi-fit while they were travelling to the Los Angeles Olympic Games, a journey of a month.

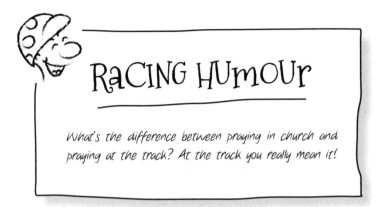

RaCING HUMOUr

What's the difference between praying in church and praying at the track? At the track you really mean it!

BY ROAD

One of my favourite stories about racehorse transport concerns Elis. In 1836 it was known that Lord Lichfield's horse was in Goodwood, Sussex, so, given that horses still walked from venue to venue, it would be 'impossible' for Elis to be in Doncaster, 200 miles away, for the St Leger four days later. Naturally, his odds lengthened.

Elis was trained by John Barham Day in Hampshire where another of his owners was Lord George Bentinck and he bet £1,000 on Elis at 12-1. His lordship was 'in the know', for he had commissioned the building of a padded, wooden horsebox on wheels, into which Elis was loaded, and he was drawn to Doncaster by a team of six carriage horses who were replaced daily by fresh ones. He duly won the St Leger.

Today horses are transported by road in vehicles that are designed aerodynamically with the well-being, safety and comfort of horses catered for; they include every conceivable luxury for both horses and attendants. They can carry up to twelve horses, but small two-horse boxes will also be luxurious, with padded walls, padded partitions, and air conditioning. Some may include a horse shower, a camera and monitor and others may even come with a horse urine waste tank fitted beneath the floor. The ramp will probably be hydraulic, and there are likely to be roof vents and an extractor fan.

The day or living quarters for grooms will include fully equipped kitchen, power, generator, luxurious upholstery, shower, electric flushing toilet, water heater, TV and DVD player – all a far cry from the early days.

BY RAIL

The advent of railways in England in 1825 transformed horse transport, although given the story of Elis (above) probably not in the early years. Most racecourses had railway stations beside them. I remember a horse called Protection running at the long gone Wye, Kent. He was near the back of the field when a train came blasting up behind him; the horse bolted and won the race. Cheltenham still has a railway siding although the days of horses being taken to the races, or hunting, by train are long gone. However, I remember my mother's first point-to-pointer, Buachalan Buidhe, arriving by train from Ireland to Tunbridge Wells West Station, itself now a shopping and business park. The Kentish bookmakers used to have great fun with his name, the most usual pronunciation being something like Buch Alan Buddy. I believe it means Yellow Boy (or possibly ragwort) in Irish.

11

MISCELLANEOUS

THE FOINAVON FENCE

In November 2013 I joined some thirty or so Grand National enthusiasts to commemorate perhaps the most unexpected winner of them all, Foinavon. We were in the Berkshire village of Compton at the now disused stables where Foinavon was trained and is buried.

It was in 1967 that Foinavon, trailing at the back of the field, was the only horse to get over the 23rd fence at the first attempt. Up ahead of him two loose horses had run across the jump as the rest of the field was approaching, and caused a massive melee.

John Buckingham, seeing the chaos, steered Foinavon to the wide outside, popped over and completed the rest of the course in splendid isolation, to win at 100–1. One or two remounted horses did their best to catch him, but in vain.

Trainer John Kempton and jockey John Buckingham were present as the plaque was unveiled in 2013. Grand National winning jockey Marcus Armytage, who scored in record time on Mr Frisk in 1990 and former champion jockeys Graham Thorner and Stan Mellor were among the gathering.

Stan Mellor had been on the fairly well fancied The Fossa but found himself deposited on to the top of the fence. He was the only one who didn't find his horse afterwards. He thought he saw The Fossa and ran to the Canal Turn to catch him and remount, only to discover it was the wrong animal.

When Foinavon was trained at Compton he had a goat for company and that went to Aintree with him. The trainer did not as he was riding another of his charges, Three Dons, at Worcester – at least he won. John Kempton later quit racing to run diving boats.

Stable lad Clifford Booth led up Foinavon and after letting him go to canter to the start, he joined the tote queue to put a sentimental bet on his charge, but he was still queuing when the tapes went up, so was unable to put anything on.

Until that day commentators only ever referred to the 23rd as 'the fence after Becher's'. Since then it has been 'the Foinavon fence'.

Nigel Payne, Aintree Press Officer, has many memories, including the following: Aintree Episodes of Channel 4's *Sunday Brunch* and *My Big, Fat Gypsy Wedding* programmes were filmed at Aintree in 2014. This was during the twenty-fifth year of Lord Daresbury's Chairmanship during which time the whole face of Aintree has changed. Winning National jockeys from the twenty-five years paid tribute to Daresbury on Crabbies Grand National day to mark his retirement. 2014 was the first £1 million National.

To commemorate a local sponsor the following facts were uncovered.

1. The Beatles played The Aintree Institute 31 times, a stone's throw away from Aintree Racecourse, located behind The Black Bull pub.

2. 50 years ago, on Tuesday 11 February 1964, The Beatles travelled from New York to Washington to play their first ever concert in North America. In 2014 the Weights were unveiled for the first Crabbie's Grand National.

3. The Casbah Coffee Club, synonymous with The Beatles, was founded as a result of horse racing. A lady called Mona Best was the first woman in Liverpool to ever be given a mortgage in her own name. She raised the money by pawning the family jewellery and placing a bet on a horse ridden by Lester Piggott. The horse won. Her winnings help set up the Casbah Coffee club where The Quarrymen played 44 times before becoming The Beatles in 1960. Without Mona Best and horse racing, popular culture could have run a very different course indeed.

4. On Monday 11 February 1963, again the day of the announcement of the Weights, The Beatles recorded their debut album, *Please Please Me*, in its entirety . So, guests were having the drinks reception in Studio 2, 51 years on to the day. (Courtesy of Nigel Payne, Aintree Press Officer)

No horses were seriously injured in 2014 for the second year in a row. A great tribute to the sophisticated safety measures introduced after the 2013 event. The new pliable core inside the fences may well be responsible for this:

THE NATIONAL THAT NEVER WAS

The 'National That Never Was' was vividly recalled by Chris Simpson:

> So much has been said and written about the 1993 Grand National which famously became known as 'The race that never was'. As far as I am concerned the reason the race failed was down to a combination of administrative error, protestors, human failing and downright bad luck.
>
> The day started badly. *My Sporting Life Grand National Edition* did not contain the Grand National pull out so I had to buy the paper twice. I was watching the race on my own for the first time (Bizarrely the only other National I tried to watch on my own was 1997 – I always make sure I have company now). I wondered why the horses had got to the start so early, ten minutes ahead of schedule. After ten minutes of walking around in the wet, patience was wearing thin and the tape which had been blowing in the wind was beginning to ominously sag, weighted down by the rain that was lashing relentlessly on the runners and riders. The starter Keith Brown finally calls the horses into line and for one brief moment it looks as if they are ready to go. Brown is just about to pull the lever and shout 'come on' when suddenly some of the jockeys stand up in their stirrups and start pointing down the course. In an instant the horses are asked to back off from the starting gate and take a turn. The BBC chose not to let us know the reason for the delay but it was fairly obvious. We had seen this before in 1991 – animal rights protestors, a small dedicated but deluded band of people who despise all that the National (and horse racing in general) stands for. In a crude attempt to disrupt proceedings some protestors had invaded the course by the first fence. It takes another ten minutes for the Police to clear the course. The jockeys get wetter, the horses more

irritable, the crowd more impatient. The atmosphere is more like that of a bear pit with the crowd baying for action. Two of the runners, Chatham and Royle Speedmaster have clearly had enough. Chatham, on the inside is digging his heels into the turf and is refusing to move; Royal Speedmaster is anxiously turning on the spot. Brown's biggest mistake of the day was not to let the horses go there and then but remember this was his last National start before retirement and he wanted it to look good. He keeps them waiting for what seems an eternity. When he finally pulls the lever the tape snags and catches the chin of Direct. To the boos of the crowd he waves his red flag and announces a false start.

By now I was on the edge of my seat. The first recall actually makes good viewing. Won't Be Long Gone and Latent Talent both get to the first fence (ironically this proves to be the nearest they will get to it), others don't get so far. 'They're being called back with commendable ease,' says the BBC's Peter O'Sullevan. Another wait, the crowd are baying for blood now, when will this race start? Finally after another excruciating wait they're 'off'.

But no – 'it's a recall'. By now my nerves have completely gone and I am in the kitchen, no doubt sitting with my head between my legs. By the time I had got my breath back and had returned to the TV I could see that the field were approaching the first fence. 'They're going to jump the first, they're going to,' cries O'Sullevan. I didn't even realise there was a problem at first. I couldn't see the tape wrapped around Richard Dunwoody's neck. I didn't notice the smaller than usual field jumping the first fence. It is not until they jump the fourth fence and John Hanmier says, 'I don't know why they're going on, it's not a race' that I realise we've had another false start and this won't count. My world collapses around me.

Thirty had started, nine remained at the start. Dunwoody was in the process of being garrotted by the tape. What was not around Dunwoody's neck was wrapped around the legs of Travel Over who comes to a painful stop after jumping the first. By the time they jump Becher's only one horse has fallen, an outsider Farm Week at the fourth fence. Once one has gone we were at the point of no return. Sure Metal and New Mill House dispute the lead with Romany King and Cahervillahow.

Party Politics is 'handy' at the Canal Turn. Fortunately falls are few, the fancied Royal Athlete comes down at the ninth, outsider Senator Snugfit at the tenth Quirinus, the poor Slovakian raider is about two fences behind. As the runners thunder back onto the racecourse for the first time no one knows quite what to do. Surely the race must be stopped? How hard would it have been to put a cordon around the Chair? A line of security guards by the water? The Aintree executive in their wisdom placed two traffic cones on the take off side to the Chair which could and were easily brushed aside by the leaders.

Now I am no rider. I haven't sat on a horse for over twenty-five years and my riding experience was limited to being led around on ponies at church fetes. It is therefore possibly unfair of me to criticise the heroic National jockeys risking life and limb for my entertainment. But – surely the jockeys still going realised something was wrong? Surely they heard boos instead of cheers as they jumped the water? Did they not see nine horses and riders milling around at the start, trainers and stable staff frantically looking for their horses? Fortunately some did notice all this and several pulled up including all of the most fancied runners, Captain Dibble and Peter Scudamore, Garrison Savannah, the hot favourite Zetas Lad, Party Politics and all the horses at the rear, Stay on Tracks, David's Duky, Direct, Mister Ed and the tailed off Quirinus. But some went on. Maybe I can sympathise with Seamus O'Neill, the rider of Sure Metal and Andy Orkney (ironically a qualified optician) on Howe Street. These were journeymen jockeys, rarely in the spotlight. This was their moment of glory, they were leading at halfway in a Grand National and were still going well. What about all those that followed? Those that turned a blind eye to the mayhem. Look at the video of the race as the horses cross the Melling Road for the second time, look at the jockeys standing up in their irons looking around them. Have you ever seen that in a 'normal' National ? No – neither have I.

In all fourteen horses went on, Howe Street, Sure Metal, Cahervillahow, Romany King and Adrian Maguire having his first ride, Esha Ness (holding my each way slip), Givus a Buck, On the Other Hand, Interim Lib and The Committee with in rear, Laura's Beau, Paco's Boy, Bonanza Boy, Joyful Noise and The Gooser.

At the twentieth Howe Street and Sure Metal are punished for leading the field a merry dance as they crash to the floor. Joyful Noise refuses and Paco's Boy is also down followed by the tailed off The Gooser at the twenty-first. 'They're sensing something's wrong but none of them are game enough to pull up,' calls Jim McGrath as they reach the twenty-third. It is too late. They couldn't stop now. Interim Lib unseats his rider at the Canal Turn and a tailed off Bonanza Boy refuses at Valentines. There are six left in with a chance, Romany King and The Committee with Esha Ness tucked closely behind. John White, riding a perfect waiting game, touches down over the last in the lead and draws clear of the fast finishing Cahervillahow with Romany King third, The Committee fourth, Givus a Buck fifth, On the Other Hand sixth and Laura's Beau a distant seventh. No desperate finish, no punching the air for White. All in all it is a little subdued. Then the 'anguish' on John White's face as he pulls up. I used to feel sorry for White – I am not sure if I do now.

Before the recriminations one must remember that no one died, only eight horses fell and all returned home safely. The television afterwards makes gripping viewing and I have managed to watch it again. I am perhaps one of the few people who did not erase their recording in disgust. I cannot watch the start as the wait is too torturous but the rest is just about bearable. A bemused Des Lynam tries to make sense of what is going on.

So who was to blame for the biggest disaster in Grand National history? Recall man Ken Evans (paid £25 for his day's work) and Keith Brown (or 'Captain Cock-up' as he was to become known) took most of the flack in the media. The Captain certainly should have let them go sooner the first time but the second time his flag didn't unfurl. Ken Evans waved the flag the first time but not the second but then if the starter's flag did not unfurl he couldn't see it. Why were the horses at the start so early? Animal rights protestors? The National is one of the country's leading sporting occasions yet it was easy for protestors to get onto the course and disrupt the race. This had happened before the start in 1991. Had no lessons been learnt?

FIDDLERS PIKE (1994)

Fiddlers Pike had won the John Hughes Grand National Trial at Chepstow the previous year. However, he was a little old to be making a National debut (thirteen) and his rider was a 54-year-old vet's wife. An early bath looked on the cards. However, keeping out of trouble in a race with some considerable grief they jumped into contention at the nineteenth fence and for one brief moment it looked as if the impossible was possible. Reality set in after Becher's second time but they still managed to finish an incredible fifth place, an astonishing achievement.

BOBBY JO (1999)

In 1999 Bobby Jo won the Grand National having been allotted only 9st 7lbs, with the talented Paul Carberry riding. He had to carry the minimum of 10st so was 'out of the handicap', yet he landed a useful gamble.

Today, with easier fences and a better class of horse contesting the race generally, it can quite often be that horses allotted between 10st and 10st 7lbs won't even get into the race, because the calibre has improved so much that the now minimum of forty horses starting may all be higher weighted.

THE MILLENNIUM

When the Millennium came in, traditional New Year's Day meetings were almost universally not held – for one thing, jockeys protested that they wanted to celebrate along with the millions of others on such a memorable date.

Just one course in Britain, Ireland and the whole of Europe took the gamble and staged a card. Its reward came when 10,000 people crammed through the gates into the small course of Waterford and Tramore, generally known as Tramore, a seaside resort on the south-east coast of Ireland.

The manager, Sue Phelan, said, 'We had taken a big gamble to stage the meeting when so many other tracks had opted to defer their fixture, but as soon as the tapes went up for the first race and I heard the deafening roar from the stands, I knew we had made the right decision.'

By coincidence, the name of the first winner was No Problem.

TRAMORE

Tramore was in the news again two years later when it became the first Irish course to use the euro. Back in 1971 it had also been the first to introduce decimalisation.

'ARKLE COINS'

The old Irish currency featured different animals on one side of a coin and the picture on a half crown (2s 6d) was of a rather fine looking horse. A friend of mine from County Galway, Tom Walshe, tells me a couple of guys took a stash of them to Cheltenham, and sold them as being of Arkle for five guineas each. When someone asked them what the 2s 6d stood for, quick as a flash up came the answer, 'It's Irish for miles and furlongs.'

12

LITERATURE

Wander into any second-hand bookshop and there are bound to be some old racing gems there; and in any current book shop there will be many modern ones. If you're lucky enough to be invited into the home of an ardent racing fan the chances are you will see rows of racing books, old and new, on their bookshelves.

Here are some of my favourites.

MEN AND HORSES I HAVE KNOWN

Written by the Hon. George Lambton (1963), it is in the charming style of its day and is a veritable who's who of top horses and men at the turn of the nineteenth century into the twentieth.

Lambton also writes about his own exploits in the saddle as an amateur, and later as a trainer. As a spectator, he would watch the races from the back of his hack, as was the custom of the time.

He was a personal friend of Fred Archer (see page 78). Many of the nobility of the day assumed pseudonyms for racing, as did any female owner who invariably went down as 'Mr' followed by a fictitious surname. One of the most colourful of the time was 'Mr Manton', in reality Caroline, Duchess of Montrose.

THE GRAND NATIONAL

David Hoadley Munroe's book *The Grand National* (1931) details all the runnings of the great race up until that time and is a must for any aficionado.

THREE MODERN MUST-HAVES

Three modern books that deal with horses from days gone by are *The Byerley Turk* by Jeremy James; *Eclipse* by Nicholas Clee and *Foinavon* by David Owen. Foinavon's story is still within the memory of many, and David Owen's account of his win in the 1967 Grand National when all the other horses were brought to a standstill at the fence after Becher's Brook is well researched and told with clarity.

The fence, the 23rd on the second circuit where the melee occurred, is actually the smallest on the course. It was re-named the Foinavon fence from 1968.

The Byerley Turk is the in-depth and thoroughly researched and fascinating story of the first founder of the thoroughbred (see page 16).

The story of *Eclipse* (2009) begins in the eighteenth century. Unbeaten in eighteen races, almost half of them walkovers, he went on to become one of the greatest sires in the history of horse racing; today 95 per cent of racehorses are male-line descendants of his. It is an interesting story, well researched and told, and an insight to the social goings on of the time, high and low.

Eclipse ran in the days when there were several heats to races, often of 4 miles, followed by a final, all on the same afternoon. Apart from his prowess as a racehorse and stallion, he is also remembered for his distinctive white face and white stocking on his off-hind leg – and especially for the saying, 'Eclipse first and the rest nowhere', a phrase which has gone down in betting history.

BROWN JACK

Written by R.C. Lyle, *Brown Jack* (1934) tells the story of possibly the most popular flat racehorse ever; it has the added bonus of illustrations by Lionel Edwards.

DID YOU KNOW?

Admiral John Henry Rous, 1795-1877, was not only a leading naval officer who saw action at sea many times, but also a leader in the world of horse racing. His father, John Rouse, 1st Earl of Stradbroke, ran a stud in Suffolk and won the 1815 St Leger with Tigris. Admiral Rous, the Earl's second son, became a steward of the Jockey Club in 1838 for some 40 years, and public handicapper in 1855 in which role he introduced the weight-for-age scale still in use universally today. He also wrote *On the Laws and Practice of Horse Racing*, and worked tirelessly to clean up racing during its darkest years of the mid-nineteenth century. He was elected a Conservative MP for Westminster and in 1863 he was promoted to Admiral on the Retired List.

RED RUM

Red Rum, Ivor Herbert's full and extraordinary story of a horse of great courage (1974) has stood the test of time; it takes the reader through Red Rum's extraordinary story up to the second of his unique three Grand National wins.

Red Rum ran in low-grade sprints on the flat as a two year old; paddled in the sea which cured a foot problem, and overcame many adversities to become a household name (Once, when I had broken a collar bone in an Essex point-to-point, we were parked outside the hospital complete with horse and trailer when some little boys in the street peered inside and said, 'Ooh, who've you got in there, Red Rum?').

He was trained from a small yard in Southport, Lancashire, and worked on the beach; former taxi driver Ginger McCain was the fifth and final trainer of Red Rum who was bred in Ireland by Martyn McEnery in County Kilkenny.

Red Rum ran in the National five times, winning in 1973, 74 and 77; he was second in the intervening two years, to Rag Trade and L'Escargot. He is buried by the winning post at Aintree, and a Philip Blacker-sculpted statue of him takes pride of place by the Aintree paddock. In terms of Grand National form, Manifesto in the 1890s, in my view, is the only other horse to come close to him.

HISTORICAL FAVOURITES

My two favourite historical racing books are *Between the Flags, A History of Irish Steeplechasing* by Colonel S.J. Watson (1969), and *The History of Steeplechasing* by Michael Seth-Smith, Peter Willett, Roger Mortimer and John Lawrence (1966).

John Lawrence later became Lord Oaksey; he was a noted amateur rider and on a horse called Carrickbeg was pipped to the 1966 Grand National post by Ayala. He was instrumental in the founding of the Injured Jockeys Fund and a truly lifelike statue of him now stands outside the IJF's Oaksey House rehabilitation centre in Lambourn.

JOHN HISLOP

John Hislop was a top amateur rider, being champion flat amateur thirteen times; he also rode under National Hunt Rules with success, and finished third in Caughoo's 1947 Grand National on Kami.

He is also the author of a number of acclaimed books. His *Steeplechasing* 1982 became the 'how-to' Bible for aspiring steeplechase riders. His *The Theory and Practice of Flat Race Riding* did the same for prospective flat race jockeys, and he also wrote *From Start to Finish*, and *Racing Reflections*, excerpts from his *Observer* newspaper column (1955). Like some of his other books, it is beautifully illustrated by John Skeaping.

In one column, in April 1951, he is berating the then Chancellor of the Exchequer, Hugh Gaitskell, for imposing an entertainment tax on horse racing, but not on football.

Horse racing, he argued, is the only sport to make a sizeable contribution towards the export trade. More than half a century on, there must be many who still share his sentiment.

In another article, in December 1950, he called for the abolition of 3-year-old hurdle races over 1½ miles, calling them, 'mad scrambles, which do not improve horses, encourage a "butcher-boy" method of riding, and seldom bear much relation to performances of the future'.

Recalling one such race with thirty-six runners, he said it was a, 'positive danger both to horses and riders, and presented a far from pleasing spectacle'.

In an article of 1954 he extols the abolition, at last, of these races. 'No rider would regret their passing,' he wrote.

John Hislop achieved his life's aim of breeding a top-class flat racehorse and, through diligent homework and with modest outlay, he and his wife bred Brigadier Gerard, winner of seventeen of his eighteen races from two to four years. In the 1971 2,000 Guineas 'The Brigadier' beat Mill Reef, who went on to be a great Derby winner.

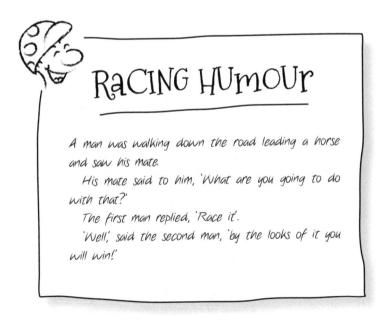

RaCING HUmOUr

A man was walking down the road leading a horse and saw his mate.

His mate said to him, 'What are you going to do with that?'

The first man replied, 'Race it'.

'Well,' said the second man, 'by the looks of it you will win!'

His only defeat came at four years, by the then current Derby winner Roberto in the Benson and Hedges Gold Cup.

John Hislop's biography of his great horse, *The Brigadier* (1973) whose talent reverberated through the early 1970s, is a must for any racing fan's book shelves.

BIOGRAPHIES

On the human biography front, *Vincent O'Brien* takes a lot of beating; it was written by his wife, Jacqueline O'Brien, and Ivor Herbert, and published by Bantam Press in 2005. Vincent O'Brien broke so many training records from humble beginnings, firstly dominating National Hunt racing with the likes of Cottage Rake (three Cheltenham Gold Cups), Sir Ken (three Champion Hurdles), Hard Knock (Gold Cup); numerous Gloucestershire Hurdle winners at the Festival, and three consecutive Grand National winners in Early Mist, Royal Tan and Quare Times from 1953-5 – and as if that pinnacle wasn't enough he went on to achieve global heights on the flat. He nurtured some of the very best in flat history like Sir Ivor and Nijinsky and many others, all chronicled in this treasure of a book.

SOCIETY

For the story of a racecourse, of social mores – and of course fashion – through the centuries, the late Dorothy Laird's *Royal Ascot* (1976) is an excellent work. Dipping in at random, I came upon the account of an incredible storm that stopped racing, exclusive tents opened up to all as people scurried for shelter, and one man, sheltering under a bookmaker's umbrella, was killed by lightening. It was Royal Hunt Cup day, 1930.

HORSE RACING FICTION

Nor must we forget racing fiction, in particular the phenomenal Dick Francis. It was a piece of racing history that was more like fiction than truth that started Dick Francis on his literary way, not long after the Queen Mother's Devon Loch sprawled halfway up the run in with the 1956 Grand National at his mercy.

As a little girl on a Pony Club outing to his stables at Fairlawne, near Plaxtol, Kent, he was introduced to us as 'the horse who didn't win the Grand National'.

Dick Francis wrote more than forty racing thrillers all told, with much of the research undertaken by his wife, Mary. Their son, Felix, took over his father's pen (OK, computer).

DOPED

The Fairlawne stables of trainer Peter Cazalet were subject to far more serious visitors in the 1950s, when a doping gang tried to inveigle their way in, as recorded by Jamie Reid in his book *Doped*. This book was short-listed for the 2013 British Horse Racing Book of the Year Award, as was *Foinavon* (see above), along with my own *Arkle, The Legend of Himself* and two others. The winner was Brough Scott's biography of the late Sir Henry Cecil, entitled *Henry Cecil Trainer of Genius*.

ARKLE, THE LEGEND OF HIMSELF

Arkle was pure pleasure to write about and very rewarding to unearth new stories and to meet so many of the people who were involved with him in the 1960s when he bestrode the steeplechasing world like a benign colossus.

As Jim Dreaper, son of Arkle's trainer, Tom, has said, Arkle's three Cheltenham Gold Cups were comparative child's play, being run on a level playing field. His extraordinary talent was proved in the handicaps in which he was almost always giving between 2½ and 3 stone to good horses.

The handicapping rules were changed in Ireland, followed by England, because of him: one set of weights to be used if he ran, with him on the top and the rest bunched together down the bottom; and the second if he didn't run, in which the remaining horses were allotted weights they could normally expect when competing against each other.

Arkle remained unbeaten over fences in Ireland – including a remarkable effort in the 1964 Irish Grand National carrying 12st from the very useful Height O'Fashion on 9st 12lbs. He was beaten in only four steeplechases; the last when he had a broken bone in his foot, the first when he slipped on landing over the third last in the Hennessy at Newbury, finishing third behind Mill House (the only time the 'Big Horse' ever beat him) and twice when he was given just too much weight even for him; even so he finished second and third.

In April 2014 a beautifully crafted bronze sculpture of Arkle and Pat Taaffe was unveiled in Ashbourne, County Meath, close to where he was trained. Sculpted by Emma MacDermott, it captured both horse and man perfectly, and is on permanent display in Ashbourne's main street, which was covered in the gold and black bunting of Arkle's racing colours for the occasion.

The project had been three years in the making and was unveiled on the day Arkle had been born fifty-seven years before. It seemed that most of the town turned out for the ceremony, along with Arkle fans from all corners of Ireland and a good few from England as well. Superbly organised by Tom Dreaper's granddaughter Lynsey, it was unveiled jointly by Jim Dreaper and Tom Taaffe, respective sons of Arkle's trainer and jockey.

OTHER REFERENCES

The Bible and Shakespeare have references, if somewhat tenuous, to horse racing.

BIBLE

Jeremiah 12:5
If you have run with the footmen, and they have wearied you, then how can you contend with horses? And if in the land of peace, in which you trusted, they wearied you, then how will you do in the jungle of the Jordan?

Luke 1:37
For with God nothing shall be impossible.
Spurgeon says that Horses of Prayer travel on this road of faith between a soul

and the very throne of God!
Here are two interpretations of that verse:

Friend, it may be the deepest wintertime in your life,
the biting frost may afflict you, the wind may be howling
around your ears
and a storm may be raging in your midst
but if you are travelling on the road of faith
 – your horses of prayer are galloping with the answer to your
prayer need –
this very moment!

Keep your road of faith open don't blockade your road with
unbelief or disobedience
or wrong living for how then will be able to communicate with
the Great King
if your horses of prayer cannot travel on the road of faith?

Exodus 14:23
And the Egyptians pursued, and went in after
them to the midst of the sea, even all Pharaoh's
horses, his chariots, and his horsemen.

SHAKESPEARE
Racing is mentioned in Shakespeare's *Cymbeline* (Act III
Scene II):

I have heard of riding wagers,
Where horses have been nimbler than the sands
That run i' the clock's behalf.

Burton, too, who wrote at the close of the Shakespearian era,
mentions the ruinous consequences of this recreation, 'Horse
races are desports of great men, and good in themselves, though
many gentlemen by such means gallop quite out of their fortunes.'

Sonnet LI
Thus can my love excuse the slow offence
Of my dull bearer when from thee I speed:
From where thou art why should I haste me thence?

Till I return, of posting is no need.
O! what excuse will my poor beast then find,
When swift extremity can seem but slow?
Then should I spur, though mounted on the wind,
In winged speed no motion shall I know,
Then can no horse with my desire keep pace.
Therefore desire, (of perfect'st love being made)
Shall neigh, no dull flesh, in his fiery race;
But love, for love, thus shall excuse my jade-
Since from thee going, he went wilful-slow,
Towards thee I'll run, and give him leave to go.

DID YOU KNOW?

It was not until 1986 that television coverage of races was permitted in betting shops. When betting shops were first allowed in 1961 they had to be behind blacked-out windows. Food and drink were strictly forbidden, and opening hours were limited.

Suluk, trained by Reg Hollinshead, became an all-weather specialist; he won 26 times, including many over all-weather hurdles and became an unfashionable stallion. He ran at Southwell thirty-nine times, just over half of them in selling and claiming hurdles, during the brief period when all-weather jumping existed. One of my favourite horses was by him; I called him Sir Luke and harboured hopes of winning a Cheltenham Gold Cup with him, convinced that he would inherit the toughness and stamina of his father. He became a hunter in Ireland.

13

TOP RACEHORSES

THE TOP-RATED FLAT HORSES

Horse	Born	Rating
Frankel	2008	147
Sea Bird	1962	145
Brigadier Gerard	1968	144
Tudor Minstrel	1944	144
Abernant	1946	142
Ribot	1952	142
Windy City	1949	142
Mill Reef	1968	141
Dancing Brave	1983	140
Dubai Millennium	1996	140
Harbinger	2006	140
Sea The Stars	2006	140
Shergar	1978	140
Vaguely Noble	1965	140
Generous	1988	139
Pappa Fourway	1952	139
Reference Point	1984	139
Alleged	1974	138
Alycidon	1945	138
Celtic Swing	1992	138
Cigar	1990	138
Daylami	1994	138
Exbury	1959	138
Nijinsky	1967	138

THE TOP-RATED STEEPLECHASERS

Horse	Born	Rating
Arkle	1957	212
Flyingbolt	1959	210
Sprinter Sacre (still in training)	2006	192
Mill House	1957	191
Kauto Star	2000	191
Desert Orchid	1979	187
Dunkirk	1957	186
Burrough Hill Lad	1976	184
Moscow Flyer	1994	184
Long Run (still in training)	2005	184
Master Oats	1986	183
Denman	2000	183
Captain Christy	1967	182
Carvill's Hill	1982	182
See More Business	1990	182
Best Mate	1995	182

DID YOU KNOW?

The Plate was the first with a set of Rules, for example:

Every rider that layeth hold on, or striketh any of the riders, shall win no plate or prize ... Whosoever winneth the plate or prize shall give to the Clerk of the Course twenty shillings, to be distributed to the poor both sides of Newmarket, and twenty shillings to the Clerk of the Race for which he is to keep the course plain and free from cart roots ... No man is admitted to ride for this prize that is either a serving man or groom.

(www.newmarketracescourses.co.uk)

Azertyuiop	1997	182
Kicking King	1998	182
Well Chief	1999	182

THE TOP-RATED HURDLERS

Horse	Born	Rating
Night Nurse	1971	182
Monksfield	1972	180
Istabraq	1992	180
Persian War	1963	179
Comedy of Errors	1967	178
Le Sauvignon	1994	178
Lanzarote	1968	177
Limestone Lad	1992	177
Bula	1965	176
Birds Nest	1970	176
Golden Cygnet	1972	176
Big Buck's	2003	176
Salmon Spray	1958	175
Sea Pigeon	1970	175
Gaye Brief	1977	175
Baracouda	1995	175

If you enjoyed this book, you may also be interested in…

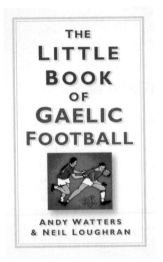

The Little Book of Gaelic Football

ANDY WATTERS & NEIL LOUGHRAN

Fact-packed and light-hearted in style, this reliable reference book and quirky guide reveals little-known facts about Gaelic football along with details of classic matches, statistical records, famous players, amusing anecdotes, and a general history. This can be dipped into time and time again to reveal something new about this ancient game.

978 1 84588 806 0

The Little Book of Ireland

C.M. BOYLAN

A reliable reference book and a quirky guide, this can be dipped into time and time again to reveal something new about the people, the heritage, the secrets and the enduring fascination of this ancient country. Despite being a relatively small island on the edge of the vast Atlantic there is always something new, charming, or even bizarre to discover about the Emerald Isle – and you will find much of it here.

978 1 84588 804 6